MAN RELATIONS TO GOD

TRACED IN THE LIGHT
OF
"THE PRESENT TRUTH"

BY THE

REV. JOHN KENNEDY.

DINGWALL.

The James Begg Society

THE JAMES BEGG SOCIETY

ISBN 0-9526799-0-6

This edition is a republication of the 1869 edition published by J. MacLaren of Edinburgh and printed by Turnbull and Spears.

© "The James Begg Society"
1995.

Introduction

On the subject of "Adoption" there have been very few words written by divines throughout the ages. The Westminster Confession of Faith, that timeless standard of protestantism, has a brief chapter on the subject in just over one hundred words. Here in this small volume the writer has given a fuller treatment, although he laments that his labours as a pastor curtailed him somewhat. However, what has been lost in length has been more than compensated for in clarity. What is found here in Rev. John Kennedy is a heavenly blend of doctrine and devotion, a fine example which refutes the idea that sound doctrine is dry and lifeless. Addressing man "in Christ" Doctor Kennedy writes:

> "Their soul shall be perfectly conformed to His; and their risen body shall be 'fashioned like to His glorious body.' Oh, what a consummation! How delightful to the Father! how satisfying to the sons! Before the Father shall the Elder Brother present the children all, in the beauty of His likeness. How certain and how fervent shall their welcome be from God! How sure is a mansion for each of them in the Father's house! How ravishing their bliss as they shall dwell there for ever!"

Much more is to be found in this little book, for the author ranges from a consideration of man as created, through fallen and evangelized, until he exhibits man as in Christ. The thinking of this "Spurgeon of the North" is clear and easy to follow: this book presents true spiritual fare, enough to satisfy the hungry soul. Above all things Dr. Kennedy lifts up his Master's Name and holds forth the Person of Jesus in a manner that is rare in our day and generation. How wonderfully he has given insight into the great work on the cross. Shining forth are all the offices of the Redeemer, who is Prophet, Priest and King. One thing is brilliantly clear: here is a firm grasp of the doctrines held by the Reformers, and more than that, there is here a felt praise for those truths.

Dr. Kennedy laboured as a weapon against error. His sword had the blood of heresy upon it, for he was sound in the faith and like the righteous in every generation he was "bold as a lion". He was not like the wicked who flee "when no man pursueth". If there was a Goliath he would war a good warfare against him; if a Nebuchadnezzar he would say, "I will not bow down". Like those who have given themselves unto doctrine "wholly" he was able to save both himself and those that heard him. In this book is found perhaps the best of Kennedy the theologian and the best of Kennedy the preacher rolled

Introduction

into one. The reader may judge for himself that though asleep in Jesus, he being dead yet speaketh.

The James Begg Society has great pleasure in bringing this little work into circulation again, with the hope that it will both instruct and edify the brethren. A few minor corrections to spelling and punctuation, and the addition of Subject and Scripture Indexes, are the only alterations from the original edition.

Acknowledgements

Particular thanks are due to Mr. & Mrs. W. Russell of Ayr, Mr. J. Frew of Springside, Irvine, Pastor J. North of Lewes, Dr. R. MacLeod of Edinburgh and others who love the Truth and have encouraged the work.

- The Publishers.

For further information about the Society please contact:

Mr Paul Hayden (Secretary)
67 Fford Garnedd
Portdinorwic
N. Wales
LL56 4QY.

Preface

IF a sculptor, who had moulded a head for a gigantic statue, and then laid it aside till he had fashioned a body for it, found, on attaching both, that the latter was utterly dwarfed, his feeling would be just what mine is, when I look on the title, in connection with the contents of this little book. The artist might plead that he lacked sufficient material, and time to use more even if he had it, to form the requisite size of figure; but he would sadly blunder, if he did not at once destroy his model, instead of exposing it and himself together. But though I plead guilty of the first mistake, I am still quite ready to appear to commit the second. The design in my mind was very different from the work which came at last from my hand. Though I intended a due proportion between the book and its title, amidst the pressing claims of other labours, I found I could not execute my design. But sworn to consult not my own honour, but the interests of the truth, and anxious that my views should be considered, rather than my work commended, I have ventured to publish what I have written. Let the title be regarded as indicating what I intended, and not as telling what I have done; and let my views be judged, not according to my design or execution, but as they appear in the light of Scripture.

CONTENTS

Preface ....Page vii

CHAPTER I.

MAN, AS CREATED, IN RELATION TO GOD.

Man as Created—Man's Original Relations to God, as Creator, Sovereign, and Judge—Man's Federal Relation to God—Was the Creator, as such, his Father?..Page 11

CHAPTER II.

MAN, AS FALLEN, IN RELATION TO GOD.

Man Fell by an act of Sin—Man an Excuseless Suicide—Spiritually Dead—An Alien and Enemy—Fallen Man under the Covenant of Works—Elect Sinners in Relation to God,...............................Page 27

CHAPTER III.

MAN, AS EVANGELIZED, IN RELATION TO GOD.

This New Relation must consist with those Previously Existing—The Peculiarity of the Gospel Dispensation—The Five Great Facts of the Gospel—Relation of Sinners, as Evangelized, to God, to Christ, to the Atonement, to Salvation,..Page 35

CHAPTER IV.

MAN, AS IN CHRIST, IN RELATION TO GOD.

The Relation Threefold—Regeneration—Relation of the Regenerated to the Spirit, to the Son, to the Father—Justification—An act by God the Judge—A Blessing from God the Sovereign—Its Object, Ground, Elements, and Effects—Adoption, its Place, its Object, its Effect—Does it Constitute a Sonship Identical with Christ's? ....Page 61

Index To Subjects...Page 83
Index To Scripture References ....Page 86

CHAPTER I.

MAN, AS CREATED, IN RELATION TO GOD.

MAN AS CREATED—MAN'S ORIGINAL RELATIONS TO GOD, AS CREATOR, SOVEREIGN, AND JUDGE—MAN'S FEDERAL RELATION TO GOD—WAS THE CREATOR, AS SUCH, HIS FATHER?

THE earth was of God for man (PSA. 115:16); and the Creator, who alone could do so, has described its genesis. Winged creatures, ambitious of displaying their power of pinion, may venture into the mists that lie over earth's beginning, to indulge in flights of speculation; and burrowing creatures, anxious to prove their power of vision in the dark, may dig into the bowels of the earth, to read its history as written on its heart; but the former fly, and the latter grope, where no light from heaven shines, and both are therefore out of sight of God. He who would behold the Creator's glory, and appreciate the greatness of His work, must occupy the standpoint which has been assigned to faith. From his position in the light of Scripture, in front of the glory of Jehovah in action, let him be neither drawn nor driven. There, and only there, can he understand, that the "worlds were framed by the word of God"; that, neither in God nor apart from Him had "things which are seen" an existence, till He willed them into being; he can observe the stages of the earth's progress towards completeness as a fit place for man, and see each accession and development, and arrangement, during the process, resulting from the fiat of the Creator, as surely as the dark and shapeless mass of the earth itself at first. In the light of "Thus saith the Lord," he can see that thus did the Lord, in fashioning and furnishing the earth for man. And to his mind, impressed with the greatness of this work of God, how little, and at the same time how great, seems man, as he at last is introduced upon the scene. How small, as compared with earth's bulk, and how important, as the climax of all this display of Jehovah's power, and as bearing his Maker's image, he is the diadem wherewith He has crowned the grand result of His action!

Man was of God for himself (ISA. 43:21), and his Creator has described his genesis, as well as that of the earth, which He formed and furnished for him (GEN. 1:11). That description must be received as it is given. Its meaning is plain, and its authority is divine. Something apart from Himself who is a spirit—the dust of the ground—was instantly developed into the organisation and symmetry of a perfect human body, by an exercise of Jehovah's power. Into that body, so "fearfully and wonderfully made," God "breathed the breath of life" (GEN. 2:7), a soul in the beauty of His own image. Man thus sprung at once out of non-existence into the full development of manhood, physically, intellectually, and morally. Had we no more minute account of man's genesis than the general statement, that he was created by God, there might seem to be an opening for the wild theory of "development." But as the case stands, no one can introduce it, to explain man's beginning, without trampling inspired statements underfoot. For the *mode,* as well as the *fact*, of his formation is written in the book of God. In scripture light man is seen perfect at once. Now, mere dust lies before God, and instantly a perfect man arises in obedience to His word.

How strong is the tendency to shrink from realising the creating power of God—to evade a sense of omnipotence! Yielding to this bias, many have desired to throw back man's beginning, as well as earth's, into the mists of an indefinitely extended past, that the glory of creating power might be hid out of view, or represented only by a result, which can command no feeling either of admiration or of awe. Beside the globule, or the monad, which, to their view, is the only direct result of Jehovah's power, man can stand erect in his pride, and retain a consciousness of greatness.

The same bias leads others, who profess to receive as true the inspired account of the first man's genesis, to conceive of the presence and power of the Creator, as far removed from themselves, in their place in the progress of the race. True, we stand on the further side of about six thousand years from that act of creation by which the first man was produced. The lines of Scripture history, and the steps of Scripture genealogy, determine this to be the distance between us and the parent pair in Eden. But are we to that extent removed from the Creator's power and presence? How prone we are to yield our feeling to such an impression as this! If God is not present in a manifest exercise of His creating power beside us, if we pass not at once out of non-existence into the perfect stature and intelligence of manhood; if, instead of this, we have been developed into our present attainment by a gradual process, the steps of whose advance are singly impalpable; is not the omnipresence of God where we are, and are we not what we are because of a course of divine operation, which stretches as a line of glory across sixty centuries of providence to the place we occupy?

In front of millenniums of divine action, and in presence of Jehovah Himself, how low ought I to lay my created being as I contemplate the eternity, immensity and power of God! Amidst millions of equals, and beside other stupendous creations, how little is my space, and how wondrous the condescension of God, who finds me there, touches me with His power so tenderly, that I am not crushed beneath His hand, and fills my cup from the ocean of His goodness, without the overflowing mercy being an overwhelming flood!

Each individual man, as a distinct existence, is the creature of God. All souls are His, He is the God of the spirits of all flesh (NUM. 16:22). If "Adam was the son of God," "we are also His offspring" (ACTS 17:28). The development of the parent stock into successive generations, and of each individual in the stages of his advancement from infancy on to manhood, is the result of a process in which the power of God, however hidden, was always active. "In Him we live and move and have our being." Having been nothing till the word of His power produced us, we can do nothing except as the working of His power enables us. All the developments of our life which are not abnormal are due directly to the continued exercise of His power. We live and move in Him,—not He in us, as if we were not distinct existences—but we, with our defined individuality of being, in Him. No pantheistic haze must be allowed to lie over the relation, in which, as dependent creatures, we stand to Him who made us. He gave us our distinct individuality of being, and yet most absolute is our dependence. How impossible is independence to a created being! What power can sustain us but that which first produced us? How constant and grateful ought our recognition of that goodness to be, by the continuous outflow of which God responds to our dependence! How vile the conduct of those who ignore their Creator, and who, under the impulse of pride, rear their meanness into an attitude of independence before the eyes of Him in whom they live and move and have their being! But how ravishing the bliss of him, who, realising God as his Creator, and admiring the glory of His power and goodness, takes his place in lowly reverence at the footstool of His throne, responds with devoted loyalty to His righteous claims, leans his dependent being on divine recourses, and rejoices in the prospect of being "filled with all the fullness of God!"

How imperatively required by the conditions of his being is the creature's subjection to God! Man alone on earth is capable of revolt. He alone is endowed with reason and will. This distinguishes him from all on earth besides. If he uses this as a power of rebellion against his Maker, how monstrous the evil he hath done! And it is as mad as it is monstrous. How can he prevail against the power of Him who made him? how can he endure the result of his rebellion, when He who made him hath ceased to show him favour, and hath directed the action of His omnipotence in wrath against him (ISA. 45:9)?

Man's relation to God as that of a mere creature, considered apart from the mode according to which his existence is conditioned, is therefore marked by entire dependence and subjection.

But man is a thinking being; "for the inspiration of the Almighty hath given him understanding." This raises him high above all other specimens of God's work on earth. This elevation is to many the pedestal on which the object of their worship rests; for reason in man is their God. To this, as to a deity, are traced all the achievements of man as an intellectual being. Who gave him his reason they will not ask; for, if they did, their idol would no longer seem divine. They value it just as it hides Jehovah out of view,—as its shadow so benights their minds that in the darkness He may be ignored. But his reason as well as his being man derives from God; and for its continuance, as surely as for the extension of his life as an animal, he is entirely dependent on his Maker. As a soul, man is in closer alliance to God than other creatures. The spirit in man is therefore more dependent than even the weak and gross body in which it is encased. It must owe all its exercise and all its rest to God. It was made to serve and to commune with God. Who can sustain that spirit but He who gave it? How desolate must it be when directing its aspirations and its efforts away from God! How vile the conduct of the man who, forsaking God, goes down to bury his reason in the grossness of the animal! Between God and flesh he stands as between a living fountain and a corrupt grave. If the human soul disdains to entomb its intellect in gross flesh, and at the same time shrinks back from God, it still indicates its dependence by its advances into the world of thought outside. It cannot satisfy itself. It cannot be its own God. The normal craving of the immortal spirit is for rest in the reality and glory of God's spiritual Being, and for supplies from the resources of His infinite wisdom. It can never be at rest till it realises God, lies adoring at His footstool, as it contemplates and admires His glory, and receives in His shining light continuous accessions of satisfying knowledge. "The Word" who is God must be "the light of men" (JOHN 1:4).

But man has heart as well as mind. He has a power of feeling as well as thinking. There are affections in the depths of his soul responsive to the objects presented by his mind. These are springs of action. And he has a power of willing. He has been created capable of originating action. His thoughts and his feelings are his own. His Creator acknowledges him as a distinct agent. He speaks to him; He transacts with him; He enters into covenant with him. He recognises his capacity of originating action and on that understanding He deals with him. How that capacity consists with his entire dependence upon God we cannot comprehend; but the problem was necessarily solved in the mode of his creation. God knoweth how man, who lives, and moves, and has his being in Himself, may yet be treated as responsi-

IN RELATION TO GOD.

ble for all his acts. According to an effective divine arrangement, the action, as such, originates in man, though the power, which made him capable of originating it, is God's. Such is man, as a moral agent, that, while all the goodness found in his actions is derived from God, the action itself, with all its goodness, is regarded as man's; and all the evil that may flow from him in his conduct must be laid to his account, even though it entered into him originally from an external source.

This power of action in man cannot be left uncontrolled by his Maker. God owes it to Himself to impose His will in the form of law on such a being. He has produced this power of action in a distinct being. That moral agent must therefore not be "without law to God."

It would, indeed, be inconsistent with the conditions of man's being that he should be controlled by a law which denies to him the power of willing, or that his Maker should direct him by the guidance of unintelligent instinct. All the responsibility of man's actions would then be his Maker's. But a rational being is not to be treated as a stone, or as a plant, or as a brute. Neither is he to be treated as a God. He must therefore be placed under a moral law. Conscience in man is the acknowledgement of that subjection.

This is required not merely because of the relation constituted by creation, but also by what God is in Himself. No power can be supreme but Jehovah's. He in the eternity of His being is infinitely before, and in the immensity of His being immeasurably above, all besides. His right to homage from all created beings rests on His own infinite excellence. He cannot exercise His creating power in such a way as leaves not an infinite interval between the elevation of His own being and the highest work of His hand; and it would therefore be unrighteous to Himself not to claim the homage of all intelligent creatures.

And the tenor of the law which He imposes is determined by His own moral character. His will must be the ultimate standard of all the moral action in the universe. How dreadful would that thought be, unless we were assured that His will was according to infinite moral excellence! He is infinitely amiable, and He infinitely loves Himself. His own infinite beauty contemplated by His omniscience is the innate object of His love and the source of His eternal blessedness. This determines what His will as Sovereign must be. From every moral agent He must demand perfect love to Himself to be expressed according to a rule which He prescribes. His infinite wisdom secures that that rule shall be perfect. The moral law, summarily comprehended in the Decalogue, is the rule which He hath given, and while its claim embraces all that is due to God, its form is perfectly adapted to man's being, relations, and normal modes of action. It is holy, for it is a perfect expression of God's will; it is just, for its claims rest on God's worthiness; it is good, because to love God is to taste His blessedness.

Under this law man was originally and necessarily placed, and through whatever transitions he may pass, whatever other relations may be induced, and to whatever extent these may be modified, his relation, as under the moral law, to God as his Sovereign, must continue. Man in heaven, earth, or hell, must be under law to God. This is determined by what God has done, and by what He is. Man was originally, is necessarily, and shall be eternally, the subject of God, as his supreme King, according to the relation constituted by his being placed under the moral law.

If God, as sovereign, issues a law, He must as judge administer it. The right to judge is His as necessarily as the right to legislate. And the exercise of the one right is as imperatively required as that of the other. His law cannot be in abeyance. It is the charter of His own inalienable rights; the assertion of His own righteous claims; an expression of His love to Himself. To allow his legislation to be ineffective, to render his government a mere ostentation of justice, to refrain from the minutest oversight of all His creatures, and of all their actions, is possible only when God shall cease to love Himself, to be zealous for his own glory, or to be capable of accomplishing the ends of His moral government. There is all the guarantee for a righteous administration of His law which can be furnished by the infinite righteousness, and by the omnipresence, and omnipotence of Jehovah. "God is judge Himself" (PSA. 50:6). None else can be so. He cannot delegate the office. True He hath committed all judgement to the Mediator. But the Mediator is the Son. He is Himself Jehovah. He has all divine power, as well as divine right to judge. It is only as Mediator He receives the office of judge from God. There is no transference of it into other hands than divine. Still may we say, as we look on the Son of man on "the great white throne," "God is judge Himself." Man's relation to God as judge, is thus normal and necessary, and therefore everlasting. It does presuppose the other constituted by subjection to law, but it is coincident with it in the order of time. No rational creature can ever cease to be thus related to God. It is true, 1st, That God as Judge, may act towards man otherwise than according to the exact circumstances of his original standing before Him. God, as Sovereign, may introduce what shall modify the results that would naturally flow out of the original arrangement of man's relation to himself as judge; but the relation itself remains intact, and all God's dealings as judge must be in perfect consistency with the necessary conditions of that relation. Thus God may justify the ungodly; but this

IN RELATION TO GOD.

He doth because of having in His sovereign love found a ransom for the guilty; and nothing required, in vindication of his own character and government, by the circumstances of man's primeval relation to Him as judge, hath been left undone, and nothing done inconsistent with its essential conditions. True, 2nd, God may exercise His authority as Judge in determining finally the fate of a creature, leaving Himself no opportunity of judicial dealing in trying and condemning him, or of having his case in any form actually at His bar again; but this results from the very perfectness of His administration. The wicked may be banished finally to the place of punishment, and the righteous finally confirmed in possession of eternal life; but in both cases the relation remains, though acts of judgement are not required to indicate or assert it, and its continuance is a guarantee for the eternity, both of the weal and the woe.

It is not with an abstraction God deals when acting judicially. *Persons* must be at His bar. When He is dealing with sin it is not a crime, but a *criminal* that is before Him. Is it not so among men? A moralist may write at his lonely desk, regarding evil as an abstraction; the social reformer may denounce crime from the platform; and the preacher may declaim against sin from the pulpit; but the judge, in the court of assize, can do nothing unless a criminal is before him. As we lift our eyes to the "high and lofty One," who is on the judgement-seat, and then look on the insignificant being who stands at the bar, how dreadful sounds the voice which utters the sentence, "Thou shalt die!" How stern is the aspect of the Judge! How rigorous the justice of his dealing! How awful the punishment He hath awarded! And how prone we are to think that the Judge is hard and pitiless! He is but a worm of the dust who stands before Him. What can he have done to provoke the Most High to wrath and to deserve a doom so fearful? It is just because Jehovah is so great, and the sinning creature so mean, that the crime is such as to deserve eternal death. The sinner has dared to strive with his Maker—to bring his will into collision with that of the Most High; he has transgressed His holy, just, and good law, in the very presence of God, and before "the eyes of His glory"; he has dared to challenge God's right to reign, though His claim to the throne rests on His infinite excellence as Jehovah; he has ventured to assert His own right to reign, and he rears the meanness of the worm thronewards, in mad ambition of the place of the Supreme; he has treated the glorious name of the Holy One with contempt and enmity; he has assumed the attitude of a deicide before the being of Jehovah; and deadly hostility, to His existence, was the bitter root, in his wicked heart, from which all the sin, with which he is charged, hath sprung. Is death eternal too severe a sentence for such a crime? I cannot but be overawed by the wrath of such a Judge, but were He less rigorous I could not revere Him. The flame of His wrath serves to make more manifest the majesty of His being; and if I cannot but dread, I cannot but adore Him.

A relation, not normal and necessary, was constituted between God and man by the Adamic covenant. For there was a covenant. There was an exchange of promises between God and Adam—from God to Adam the promise of life; from Adam to God the promise of obedience; the fulfilment of the latter being the condition of the fulfilment of the former. The divine promise is not given in express terms, but it is implied in the terms of the transaction. To confine the possibility of falling to one sin, was in effect to promise life, in the event of that sin not being committed. And the terms of the threatening implied that there was a promise of life. "The commandment was ordained to life" (ROM. 7:10). Nor is man's promise to God given in express terms; but the proposal by God required, and the proposal to man as holy secured, an engagement on the part of man, to render perfect obedience to God. To refrain from the one sin, which it was possible for him to commit, was in all else to do the will of God. Thus in perfect consistency with man's dependence on God as his Creator, his subjection to God as his Sovereign, and his responsibility to God as His Judge, a new relation was formed by God, between Himself and man, with a view to a special manifestation of His own glory.

In this transaction, the first man was dealt with, as the head of all his posterity. Adam was mankind as he covenanted with God. The peculiarity of mankind, as a propagating race, was taken advantage of as an occasion for a display of the manifold wisdom of God, in dealing with a race as such, and yet with each individual of that race distinctly, so that the two processes would perfectly harmonise; the individualised providence preserving its own distinctness, as a defined current, in the midst of a course of dealing, which comprehends the family of man as a whole. Adam was constituted the federal head of all his seed. The whole race was in him before the mind of God. And Eve, the individual specimen of mankind, was beside him, and was singly dealt with. The opening chapter of providence thus gives us an epitome of the whole—a perfect sample of the wise and holy government, which shall finally be wound up in a consummation, disposing of the race in a way, that shall be to the praise of Jehovah's glory, and leaving to no individual the shadow of a reason for taking exception to the efficiency and righteousness of His reign.

The covenant of works was the result of a rightful exercise of God's sovereignty; it was admirably adapted to the unity of the race and its succession of generations; it was brightened by the glory of divine

IN RELATION TO GOD.

goodness; and, while complete in itself, it is perfectly fitted to be the introductory dispensation of providence.

The position assigned to Adam, by this covenant, determines the relation which all his race, as represented by him, hold to God. If the story of Eden seems to present to us only an individual man, it is in this form, that each child of Adam might read it as the record of his own earliest history.

Were these the only relations subsisting between man and God before the fall? Or was there between God, and man as His creature, such a relation as there is between a father and his child?

The right settlement of this question is of first-rate importance. At first sight, it may seem of little consequence to determine, whether his relation was superadded or not, if only the others are conserved; and if divine action according to those is not held to be modified by the requirements of this. But a careful consideration of the subject will discover, that it is impossible to reconcile what has been done by God, as Sovereign and Judge, with what should be expected from Him, as Father; and that it is extremely difficult to believe in a Fatherhood constituted by creation, and a salvation originating in sovereign grace. The position that no such relation was constituted by creation, is one of the outworks of Calvinism which has not hitherto been sufficiently strengthened. Those, who failed to perceive, that it was a point of importance, in conducting the defence, resigned it to their opponents, and most damaging use have they made of it.

It is necessary to determine what such a relation implies, ere we inquire whether it exists. His not doing so, at the outset, is a marked defect, in the first part of Principal Candlish's remarkable work on "the Fatherhood of God." To say that man, as created, was not the son of God, is apparently to deny an express Scripture statement. An easy triumph thus seems to be allowed, to superficial thinkers, by the want of a distinct definition of the sonship, which is denied to man. He might have proclaimed his intention to prove, 1. That creation did not constitute such a relation between God and man, as that which is formed by adopting grace, and 2. That no such relation was formed by creation, as is analogous to the relation of mutual love between a human father and his child.

Creation did constitute such a relation as subsists between a parent and his offspring (ACTS 17:28). We are declared to be the offspring of God the Creator. Adam is said to be "the son of God," in the same genealogical sense in which Seth is said to be "the son of Adam" (LUKE 3:38). But that statement merely accounts for the existence of Adam. He came immediately from the hand of God. It tells us this, but it teaches no more. There God is shown in the relation of a parent to the offspring, he produced by an act of His creating power; not as a Father, in loving relation to His child. True, the human parentage involves the fatherhood. The human parent is bound to be a father to his offspring—to love his child and to do his utmost for his good. But his relation as *parent* is not identical with his relation as *father* to his child. The one is *natural*, the other is *moral;* the one must necessarily precede the other; the one is shared in common with the brutes, the other is peculiar to moral agents; the one is determined by the law which regulates the propagation of the species, the other by the moral law of righteousness. Among men parentage requires fatherhood; but does the divine parentage, implied in the Creator's relation to man, involve an analogous fatherhood?

The conditions of the parentage are altogether different in the two cases. Man is parent and at the same time under the moral law of God. It is as under law that he is bound to be a father to the child of which he is parent. It is right, and therefore requisite, that, being the parent, he be also the father of his child. He is in such close connection with his offspring that the law, which requires him to love his neighbour as himself, must require a peculiarly fervent affection from him towards his child. They are both of the same nature and in the same rank. They are in a most emphatic sense 'neighbours,' and therefore mutual affection peculiarly intimate, and corresponding, in its expression, to their mutual relations, must be demanded from both. But how different is the case, when we turn to the divine Parent, and to man as "His offspring"! It was according to no previously imposed law that Jehovah became a Parent. He created man by a kingly word of power. He did so in the free exercise of His own sovereign will. The being, man, came at His fiat out of nothing. How different, too, the nature of man from that of God! How diverse their modes of being! How infinite the disparity of rank between them! What law could impose an obligation on Jehovah to act the part of Father to His creature? Did He not create him with a view to the manifestation of His own glory? Is He not free to deal with him in order to that end, without being restricted by any such conditions as fatherhood would impose?

The relation of fatherhood would impose conditions which cannot consist with the free exercise of God's sovereignty. Can we conceive of a father not bound, by his having or assuming the position defined by that name, to do his utmost for the security or welfare of his child? Can we conceive of a fatherly love not disposing him, in whose heart it is, to do what he can to secure his child from death and damage? If there is any reality in fatherhood it must involve this; and if there is any paternal affection it must dispose to this. And is God really the

IN RELATION TO GOD.

Father as well as the Creator, of our race, and yet acting in a way utterly inconsistent with such a relation, and with the love without which such a relation cannot be a reality? It is a relation requiring mutual love, or it is nothing. From him, who holds the father's position, it requires such love as disposes him to do his utmost for the welfare of his child. If God is Father, we must expect that disposition in infinite measure. He, as Father, cannot possibly fail to love, and to express His love in securing eternal good to His children. To ascribe to Him a fatherhood which is not thus sustained, is foully to dishonour Him. All He is, He is perfectly. There is infinite reality in His fatherhood if it exists at all. The child's place is in the father's heart and all the father's power surrounds him as he is there. I cannot conceive of "the Lord Almighty" as Father (2 COR. 6:18), without regarding it as utterly impossible that His child can die. His love disposes Him to do good to His child, and His omnipotence can accomplish all the behests of His love. But what is His way of dealing with man in Eden? He places him under trial. He makes his life dependent on the issue of that trial. He allows the liar and the murderer to approach him. He knows his deadly intent, and yet He permits the serpent to enter Eden; and He allows man to fall. He lets man die under His all-seeing eye. Can that fallen man be the child of God? The very idea is revolting.

But does fatherhood require such love and such protection? May there not be a real fatherhood without affection so fervent and patronage so effective? Was there not an exuberance of kindness in God's treatment of man in Eden, and are there not tokens of mercy yet in His providence towards man as fallen, which indicate real fatherliness on the part of God? There is indeed much in the dealing of God with His creature, to prove Him a Sovereign abundant in goodness and rich in mercy; but are the claims of *God* to *fatherhood* to be sustained by instances of goodness, which fall short of a full expression of a human father's love? Is this the kind of way in which I am to conceive of God as acting the part of a father? All the kindness traced up by some to fatherliness, should rather be ascribed to the goodness of God as King. His subject, while loyal, must know from experience how good his Sovereign is. The ravishing bliss of Eden assures innocent man of this. And his gifts, to the evil and unthankful (MATT. 5:45), are God's vindications of his goodness, to render excuseless all who rebel against Him.

If creation constituted, annihilation alone can destroy, this relation. Man, if a child, because created, must be so in all conditions and for ever. What kind of mind must that be, which can endure the idea of the divine Father contemplating so many of His children, in the midst of all the eternal woe, into which sin has plunged them!

But does not the creation of man, in His own image, constitute the relation of father to son, between his Maker and man? There is really no new element, introduced into the argument, by taking man's conformity to God into account. Adam begat a son in his own image; but it was not his likeness to his parent that made him a son. He bare his image, as his offspring, and not as his son. If God created man at all as a rational being, thus alone could he have created him. He must have been perfectly holy as he came from his Maker's hand. Once he hath been created, and the issue of the covenant of works hath been evolved after trial, then men may enter into life as sinners in perfect consistency with divine holiness. But the first man must be holy because God is holy. As coming directly from the hand of God, he could be neither unholy nor neutral. But what could there be, in his conformity to his Maker, to impose upon God the position and functions of a Father? Must God be man's Father because He made him capable of doing His will as King? To maintain this would be to insist, that the perfect adjustment, of man's relation as subject, has interfered with the full exercise of His own rights as the Sovereign.

If his being like his Maker made man a son of God, then *ipso facto* regeneration restores him to that relation. If so, there is no place at all for an act of adoption on the part of God the Father. The Spirit makes them sons by creating them anew in the image of God. Sonship would thus be a subjective thing—a condition of soul, and not the relational status of a person; not the result of an act of grace on the part of God the Father, but something implied in a work of grace performed by God the Holy Ghost!

The idea, of the salvation, which is by Jesus Christ, being a mere restoration of fallen man, is used as another argument in favour of an original sonship. If salvation is so and no more, then man in his state of innocence, must have been a son of God, for undoubtedly "to as many as received Him" Christ "gave power to become the sons of God" (JOHN 1:12). But is salvation merely a restoration of man to his primitive state? That there must be restoration cannot be denied. But is this all? Of course the saved must be restored to likeness unto God; but does not this secure to them in Christ capacity for more blissful service, and for the enjoyment of more intimate communion with God? Of course it restores them to the favour of God; but is not the believer's footing, as accepted in the Beloved, more secure than Adam's was, and more elevated than his would have been, even if he had never fallen? Is not the infinite love of God the source of the salvation which is by Jesus Christ (JOHN 3:16)? Is not God's dealing with man through Jesus Christ intended to be "to the praise of the glory of His grace"

IN RELATION TO GOD.

(EPH. 1:6)? Is there not in the grand antecedent of God's love, in the gift of His Son, enough to compel us to expect more than mere restoration to pristine blessedness? Is not the Son the mediator? Are not the divine and human natures already united in His person? Can we refrain from expecting that those who are in Him shall attain to unprecedented nearness to God? Hath not Christ Himself told us, that He hath come and died, that His "sheep might have life" "more abundantly" (JOHN 10:10)? Is it not said that "where sin abounded, grace did much more abound" (ROM. 5:20)? Who, after carefully reading the fifth and eighth chapters of the Epistle to the Romans, will venture to say, that all which the love of God desiderates, and the Son, as Redeemer, achieves, is the mere restoration of the elect to the position, actual or prospective, which they once held in Adam?

But "what saith the Scripture"? Attempts have been made to prove, that such a relation between God and all men as requires the mutual love of father and son, is revealed to us in the word of God. But these have resulted in producing, beyond perversions of some texts, merely a few passages, referring to the relation of parent and offspring; repeated acknowledgements by God of his relation as Father to Israel as the people "to whom pertained the adoption"; and an inference from one of the Lord's parables.

Such passages as LUKE 3:38, ACTS 17:28,29, and HEB. 12:9, merely indicate such a relation, of the Creator to man, as is analogous to that of a parent to his offspring. The proper idea of *fatherhood,* as distinguished from *parentage,* is not found in any of them. And all those passages, referring to the relation between God and the nation of Israel, are not only quite irrelevant, but have, if any, a force opposed to the doctrine in support of which they are cited (PSA. 148:14; ROM. 9:4). Israel, as a people, were taken, *by a gracious act of adoption,* into a relation of peculiar nearness to God. Their being children was a distinguishing characteristic of their status, as compared to others. All the proof, of their being adopted, which can be found in Scripture, establishes the doctrine of a special fatherhood, of the God of Israel, originating in sovereign grace, and forbids the idea of a universal fatherhood; and His relation to His peculiar people, as constituted by adoption, and securing special privileges to His children, typifies that real fatherhood which He sustains towards His spiritual Israel in Jesus Christ.

The inference, in support of a universal fatherhood, from the parable of the Prodigal son (LUKE 15), is quite unwarranted. No parable should be strained to teach more than the lesson which it was intended to convey. What this is, may be learned from the occasion on which it was delivered, or from the question to which it was a reply, or from the moral educed from it by the Lord Himself. There need be no mistake as to the occasion of this particular parable. "Then drew near unto Him all the publicans and sinners for to hear Him. And the Pharisees and Scribes murmured, saying, this man receiveth sinners, and eateth with them." This occasioned the parable. The parties introduced were manifestly intended to represent the Saviour, the sinners, and the murmurers. These are the parties whose conduct it illustrates. And the types of these in the parable are easily allocated. The father represents Christ, the elder son, the murmuring scribes and Pharisees, and the prodigal son, the publicans and sinners. This is so apparent, that it is quite unaccountable how any other interpretation of the parable could be offered. The relation between the father and his prodigal son indicates *the relation of love between Christ and the sinners whom He saves.* It teaches this and no more. It throws no light on the relation in which men stand to God, for it was not intended to do so. The murmurers regarded themselves as worthy of all favour, and Christ accords to them, in the parable, the position which they claimed. They regarded the publicans as abandoned prodigals, and to them Christ gives the position which was thus assigned to them. And by the conduct of the father, in contrast to that of the elder brother, He vindicates His gracious reception of sinners, whom proud Pharisees would exclude from all favourable regard.

It is enough to show, to what shifts the advocates of a universal fatherhood are driven, that a learned professor quotes, as conclusive proof, the words used by sinners in Israel to justify their intermarriages with the heathen. "Have we not all one father?" they asked, "hath not one God created us" (MAL. 2:10)? He interprets this passage as if it read "Have we not all one father?" *for* hath not one God created us?" If he would insert a word, why not the one which the sense evidently requires; and then read the passage thus,—"Have we not all one father," *Adam?* "Hath not one God created us?"

Dr. Crawford claims support from 'the Sermon on the Mount.' He insists that Christ is there addressing a mixed multitude, and yet speaking to them as children of God; forgetting that Christ calls those whom He is addressing, "the salt of the earth," "the light of the world," and a people whom the Lord hath blessed (MATT. 5:13,14; 5:11,12).

The doctrine of the universal fatherhood of God cannot fitly or safely get a place in Calvinism. Any exercise of goodness required by the relation, which creation constitutes, between God, as Ruler, and the creature of His hand, that system does take into account. But if there is such a relation, between God and His fallen creatures, as between a father and his son, it seems utterly inconsistent, with all that conditions God's place in that relation, to make no provision for the recov-

IN RELATION TO GOD.

ery of all His children. If salvation flow from the fatherly love of God to any, it must flow to all. The return of the prodigal and his gracious reception are traced by many to this affection, which is held to have survived the fall, and to have found its characteristic expression in the restoration of the "son who was lost." Thus salvation would be accounted for, as something necessary in vindication of God's name, as the Father of His creatures. If it hath not necessarily flowed from the nature of God, it is the inevitable result of a previous course of action, in which the honour of His goodness became involved! The doctrine of the universal fatherhood of God leads so insensibly but so irresistibly to this, that a professor of theology, under vow to teach according to a Calvinistic formula, thus writes in support of it:—"May we not reasonably conclude that God, having brought such creatures into being, 'will not forsake the work of His own hands?' Having so far acted towards them as a father, in giving them existence, and imparting to them His own likeness, we cannot suppose that He will thereafter leave them orphans.

The same love which originally moved Him to the creation of them, will move Him still to watch over them with parental care, and to provide for them with parental kindness and liberality. And even when, like prodigal sons, they have departed from Him, and forfeited by their sins all title to His favour, it is no incredible thing that His fatherly love may still yearn after them, and may devise means whereby, without prejudice to the authority of His laws, and the majesty of His government, His banished ones may, if penitent, be restored to the comforts of His home and the endearments of His fellowship...?" Again he writes: "the mediatorial work of Christ" "proceeded from the unspeakable warmth and tenderness of His fatherly love."

And again, "the humiliation and sufferings of Jesus Christ were intended to manifest the fatherly love of God." In these and numerous other passages, the love of God, from which salvation flowed, is represented as fatherly love—the affection which befits the relation, in which He stands to His creatures as such. And this is the love in which salvation originated! A Father, as such, loving all His family, and providing salvation only for some of them! This is the well-spring, and such the God of salvation! This may be a necessary deduction from the doctrine of the general fatherhood; but it is directly opposed to the Word of God, which plainly teaches, that God saves sinners, not because He was the Father of any or of all; but because, as the great "I am," He will have mercy on whom He will. Salvation flows to men, not necessarily out of the divine nature, nor as a natural result of previous divine procedure, nor as a fitting expression of fatherly affection, but from the good pleasure of the Sovereign Lord of all (MATT. 11:25);

MAN, AS CREATED, IN RELATION TO GOD.

because He loves, not because He is love; because He is the Lord and has willed to love, and not because He is a Father and is bound to love.

CHAPTER II.

MAN, AS FALLEN, IN RELATION TO GOD.

MAN FELL BY AN ACT OF SIN—MAN AN EXCUSELESS SUICIDE—SPIRITUALLY DEAD—AN ALIEN AND ENEMY—FALLEN MAN UNDER THE COVENANT OF WORKS—ELECT SINNERS IN RELATION TO GOD.

MAN sinned, and by sinning fell. It was by an act of sin he fell—he ate the forbidden fruit. It is this overt act that is set before us, in scripture light, as the procuring cause of all his ruin. What occurred in the secrecy of his soul, ere sin was developed in that act, we cannot tell; for God has not unveiled it. That soul was the abode of innocence, the temple of God, and yet sin entered into it, and came forth in an act of disobedience.

In accounting for man's fall, we cannot trace the sin which procured it further back than man himself. It originated, *as an act,* in him. True, the tempter was in Eden; the "liar and murderer" was busy there. But he was weak against the will of man. He could not take the citadel of Mansoul by storm. Ere he could enter, the gates must be opened from within. This is made patent in God's description of the fall. If Satan seems to triumph, he has no ground of boasting. His is not the position of being an independent source of evil; of evil even he is not the god. He is but its slave himself, though the world submits to his power as if he were a god. He cannot show himself godlike, even when weak man is the subject on whom he operates. It is a profound mystery, and shall be so perhaps for ever, how the Holy One permitted the introduction of sin. But while I cannot but tremble, as I reflect on His mysterious connection with sin and the fall, I cannot but rejoice to recognise His effective presidency, as the Only God, even under the shade which the prince of darkness casts over the bright bliss of Eden. Satan has carried infection to the garden; and this is all his achievement. He need not boast. The wandering leper has affected another with the plague; and that other has thus become unclean like himself. His form and demeanour were those of a serpent:—so far from being godlike was he. He decoyed into fellowship with himself, in the slavery of sin, one who was once, like himself, in the image and service of God; but this is all the triumph of his power. The serpent has bitten, because man opened his bosom to receive him; and the poison has done its deadly work. But the deadly deed was man's. Satan had not the power to kill. He only tempted man to slay himself; and all the more guilty is the suicide, because he had not only all the attractiveness, of divine glory and goodness, to attach him to the service of God, but all the loathsomeness of the liar, to scare him from the evil.

The sin was committed, and God departed. With His presence all spiritual life was gone. The soul God-forsaken, is now dead. Of the soul, deserted by God, sin takes possession. Sin is now an operative principle in that soul, determining all its states of feeling, and the character of all its exercises. That principle is not dependent for its continued existence on the presence of Satan, as is the life of God in the quickened soul on the presence of the Spirit of God (EPH. 2:1-3). Nor are its motions merely the results of an impetus given by the active power of Satan. He is not the god of evil. He is himself the victim and the slave of sin; he cannot be its god. But he "keeps" that dead soul as "his palace," and he works as a "prince" in that child of disobedience.

If the principle of spiritual life is love to God, that of spiritual death is enmity to God; for there is an active principle in this death, as surely as there is in that life. Spiritual death is not mere impotence; it is not a mere negation. To be dead is to be under the sway of sin; and essentially sin is enmity to God (COL. 1:21). A rational soul cannot be neutral in relation to God. There must be infinite repulsion, in divine holiness, if it has ceased to attract. God must be either loved or hated. Fallen man must be an alien, in relation to the living God, for he is dead; and he must be an enemy, to the Holy God, for he is under the sway of sin.

All the image of God is effaced from the soul of fallen man. That temple is now an utter ruin. True there is still some light—"the work of the law written in the heart," (ROM. 2:15),—but, like a lamp, hung from the broken vault of a ruin, its flickering glimmer only makes more manifest the wreck on which it shines. True, there is a conscience still in that fallen soul, which seems as if it were a living thing amidst the dead;—the one survivor of those who once worshipped in that temple. It is there, and it speaks; but its cry, like the screech of the owl amidst the desolation of the ruin, only serves to make the place more dismal. It befits the ruin; it is no exception to its utterness. Or, if a survivor, it is so only as that maniac is, to whom the fall of the temple was the death of his reason; and who, with the life of an animal only, still haunts the scene of ruin, finding nought to feed on but the putrid carcasses of the dead, and making with his shrieks, which express alike his madness, his hunger, and his loathing, the place more dismal than if all were still.

Man, as fallen, is a dependent creature, and, at the same time, a guilty sinner. He lives in God while he is a child of wrath. He is at once sustained and accursed by God. He is upheld by His power while he is lying under His wrath.

The forbearance of God with individual sinners, though profoundly mysterious, is a necessary element of the scheme of providence, bearing on the race, and presents to us an aspect of the divine character, which could appear, only in His dealings with beings conditioned as are fallen men. It is only under the reign of One, who is long-suffering, that mankind could be propagated according to the Creator's design. And this feature of the general scheme, which embraces all, is quite consistent with perfect rectitude of dealing bearing on each individual. How God, as Judge, may regard a sinner, as obnoxious to His wrath, and meantime, as Sovereign, show him mercy, we may not be able to comprehend; but an opportunity of displaying His clemency, as King, is as necessary, in the view of God, to the due manifestation of His glory, as an occasion for exhibiting the rigour of His righteousness, as Judge. The coming judgment does not detract from the present mercy. It is all the more glorious, because extended to one, who must yet be overtaken by judgment. Nor does the present mercy interfere with the execution of the judicial sentence at the appointed time; and shall only have afforded occasion, for a more glorious display of justice, when the day of vengeance shall at last have come.

How awfully solemn is the position of a creature, who must be dependent on God, and yet cannot bear to realise this, because he hates His holiness and dreads His wrath! Receiving mercies which prolong a life spent in treasuring wrath against the day of wrath (ROM. 2:5)! Treated kindly and taking foul advantage of this goodness to harden his heart the more! Taking what comes from the hand of God, and not choosing and not daring to look up to His face! A child of wrath, conscious of immortality, standing on the edge of a moment at the brink of Eternity! Such is the condition, and such the life of man, as dependent, immortal, and sinful, in relation to God, as his Creator, Sovereign, and Judge.

But the relation, in which man, as fallen, stands to God, must be viewed in the light of the broken covenant of works. That covenant has been broken; but it is only by man. It has not ceased to be in force. Man failed to obey; and the promise of life cannot be fulfilled to him; but "God abideth faithful." He is pledged to condemn, just because He can no longer bless. There has been no covenant-breaking on God's side. Nor has there been any thwarting of God's purpose by man's transgression. Jehovah yet stands committed to the dispensation arranged by his covenant with Adam. There can be no such modification, of the conditions of that covenant, as is inconsistent with its perfectness and its perpetuity. If a new dispensation is introduced, it

MAN, AS FALLEN,

is not in order to remedy any defects in this, but to give a more glorious exhibition of God's character, such as is consistent with a perfect adherence to all its principles, and which shall secure a perfect practical regard to the minutest details of its arrangements.

And to what is God committed by the Adamic covenant?

1. He hath bound Himself for the punishment of all the sin chargeable against the race. The curse of the law requires this. Death is due for the first sin to all, and for his own sin, to each. Already accursed as a child of Adam, each sinner of the race earns for himself the death which is the wages of sin. This is the only service for which he has either heart or hand, and this the only reward to which he has any claim. "Cursed is every one that continueth not in all things which are written in the book of the law, to do them" (GAL. 3:10), is the awful sentence, which hath gone forth from the throne of judgment, and it must take effect, that justice may be satisfied (ROM. 2:3).

2. He hath bound Himself to demand perfect obedience, in order to life, from each individual of our race. His claim to perfect obedience does not rest on the terms of the covenant with Adam. This is founded on His own infinite excellence, in relation to moral agents created by Himself. What is peculiar, to the covenant of works, is not the extent of God's claim, for this must be the same under any form of administration. Perfect obedience must always be the demand of the moral law of God. The federal peculiarity is making this the condition of life. The law's claims cannot change. To adapt them to man's fallen state would be to nullify the law, as a charter of divine rights, and to limit man's responsibility by his wickedness.

How hopeless, then, is the attainment of life by man, according to the terms of the covenant of works (ROM.3:20)! He is already condemned. His only way of meeting the demands of divine justice is to resign himself despairing to eternal death. Perfect obedience is the only condition of life, proposed to him, as he lies under the reigning power of sin! There can be no abatement of the law's claims, and no mitigation of the law's curse. Under the yoke of the law, and under the power of sin, at the same time, how hopeless are his attempts to reach the goal of life! Already accursed, and always sinning, how hopeless is his deliverance from "the wrath to come"!

There is a strong tendency to hide the stern features of this aspect of our state, as sinners, in relation to God. To examine our position, in the light of the law of works, would lead to humiliation and despair; and men will cleave to self and cling to hope. They refuse to receive as true, God's account of their utter helplessness as sinners. They try to hide, from their view, the awful aspect of God's character as presented to them by the law. "Without the law," as they are (ROM. 7:8), sin lies dead, in the grave of their insensate hearts. It is there, and it is mighty and active and reigning, but to their consciousness it is as if it were dead,—as if it were not. They use another standard than God's law to try what they are, and they are sure to elect one that shall not disturb their self-complacency. To be neighbour-like, is their ambition—not to be God-like,—and thinking they succeed in being so, they are content. They ignore the God who revealed His awful glory on Mount Sinai. They think of the mercy of providence as the only appreciable exhibition of God's character. Or, they cast the veil of a universal fatherhood over the stern aspect of God's character and relation as Judge. Or, they regard the gospel as entirely superseding the law, and as introducing a new state of things in which the law is quite ignored.

1. True, there is, meantime, mercy shown to fallen sinners. This may seem, to some minds, utterly inconsistent with the terms of the Adamic covenant. It held out no prospect of any mitigation of the punishment awarded. Wrath to the uttermost is its natural outcome to fallen man. But the forbearance of God with sinners is owing to another covenant, and is the necessary prelude of "the grace which bringeth salvation." It is not an inconsistency in God's dealings; it is not incompatible with the covenant of works. If no scheme was being developed in the providence of God, but that which was introduced in His covenant with Adam, any mercy would be an inconsistency in God's dealing with our race. But there is another; and it conserves all that was required by the first. The forbearance, extended to sinners, is an exercise of God's mercy as Sovereign, reserving an opportunity for the development of the scheme of grace. In the case of all who shall find the mercy which endures for ever, all the claims of God, according to the first covenant, have been fully met by Christ; and in the case of all others, the mercy of providence shall be withdrawn at an appointed time, that justice may be satisfied in their eternal death.

2. True, man's created being is dependent on God, and He fitly responds to that dependence by a benign exercise of his power. But does this imply that the gifts received by man are tokens of a Father's love? Whatever may have been man's original relation to God, it cannot be that of a child, under the covenant of works. By its arrangements man is placed in the position of a subject, who has nothing to expect beyond what he can claim on the ground of perfect service. If he was in the heart of God, as His child, before, he must have been cast out of it ere he was placed, on such a footing as this, in relation to His King. But a child he could not have been, for if so, he never had thus been treated. Now that he is fallen, there is at any rate no opportunity for any exercise towards him of God's fatherly love. The fiction of a universal fatherhood of God, expressed to all in the kindness of

MAN, AS FALLEN,

providence, has been woven by the imagination of sinful men, as a veil by which to hide the stern glory of God's name and throne as Judge. They like to think of Him as a Father, who is indulgent to His foolish children, and to whose pity their helplessness can effectually appeal. He seems to them a Being in whom compassion is a weakness, of which advantage may be taken; instead of being regarded as a Sovereign, who, in order to the fulfilment of His purposes, and in perfect consistency with all His rigorous righteousness as Judge, is extending mercy for a season to sinners, who shall all the more miserably perish, if His goodness shall not lead them to repentance.

3. True, also, the gospel reveals a covenant of grace, according to which a free salvation, from all sin and misery, has been secured to some sinners of our race. But this involves no contravention of the covenant of works. "Salvation by grace" is bestowed on the foundation of a righteousness, by which the law, as administered according to the covenant of works, has been magnified and made honourable. The revelation of God's saving love is bright with a display of all the attributes of His character as Judge. It is not at the cross of Christ, that one can learn to suspect the perfectness of the Covenant of works; and find it possible to throw a vague idea of mercy, as a veil, over the awful glory of the God who is a "consuming fire." Christ the Son of God is crucified. Bearing the imputed sins of a people, whom God loved from everlasting, even He dies an accursed death. At the expense of His blood, God fulfils the stern word of vengeance, and at the same time, the gracious promise of redemption, proclaimed in Eden. His hatred of sin is a fire of wrath in the experience of His Son, as surety, purchasing redemption for His chosen. His name, as involved in the covenant of works, is vindicated by the shameful and awful death of "the man" who was His "fellow"; who was "upholding all things by the word of His power," when he in flesh was suspended "on the tree"; and who, on His way to the place of sacrifice, during His life in the flesh on earth, stilled by His word the tempest, healed all manner of sickness, scattered legions of devils, and raised the very dead from the grave. He who displayed such glory in the flesh, endured in the flesh all the shame and agony of an accursed death. Raising one's eye from His cross to the throne of Jehovah, how glorious in holiness He seems, who required this satisfaction for the transgressions of His people; how manifest it is, that the scheme, unfolded in the gospel, sheds the lustre of its glory on that which was embodied in the covenant of works, instead of displacing it as something imperfect or effete; and how infallibly certain it is, that wrath to the uttermost, according to the curse of the law, must be the portion of all who have not the righteousness which is by Jesus Christ.

IN RELATION TO GOD.

While all men, as fallen, are equally aliens, enemies, condemned and lost, they are not all regarded indiscriminately by God. He knows some of them as objects of His everlasting love (ROM. 9). These He loved, not because they were good, and as such to be regarded with complacency; nor because they were lost, and as such to be regarded with compassion. Nor did He love them, because He Himself was love. If that was the reason for His loving any, it must be a reason for His loving all. He loved them because He was pleased to love them. His election of some is due to a sovereign exercise of His will, as well as His not loving others (MATT. 11:25,26). Those who were before His mind as sinners not elected, He ordained, as Judge, to death for their sins; but the objects of His electing love, were as such, before His mind, neither as saints nor as sinners (ROM. 9:11).

The relation constituted by election, is one subsisting only in the mind of God. The elect, in a state of nature, are as surely as others, children of wrath, in relation to God, as Judge. They are then unconscious of, and unaffected by their election. They shall, as elect, be preserved within the reach of grace, till the set "time of love" has come; but the first gracious fruit of their election must be a change of state, by their union to Christ, that the purpose of mercy may take saving effect. For there was a purpose of mercy, determining God to a special course of action, bearing exclusively on the elect. In arranging for the fulfilment of that purpose, God contemplated them as sinners. Even those *exercises* of His love which were *immanent,* referred to them as fallen. They were so regarded, when He made a covenant with His chosen. When Christ was "set up from everlasting," as their federal Head, it was with a view to His doing and dying for them, as sinners helpless and condemned; and in order to their salvation as sinners corrupted and enslaved.

The covenant of grace introduced, in the view of God, a new relation between Him and the Elect. They are regarded as in federal union to Christ, as surely as they were in Adam when God covenanted with him in Eden. How wide, before the eye of God, is the interval which separates these from all others! They are chosen in Christ to eternal life; and their salvation is as certain as Christ is infallible; while the salvation of all others, appears, to the divine mind, an utter impossibility.

Another peculiarity is added to the relation of the elect to God, by the incarnation of the Son, their federal Head. He took hold of "the seed of Abraham" by taking their nature. He thus constituted Himself their Kinsman, their Brother. "He that sanctifieth and they who are sanctified" are thus "all of one" (HEB. 2:11). He now, not only represents them as their federal Head, but He is allied to them as "the word made flesh." He, being the Son of God and their Brother, is the medium of a peculiar relation between them and God. It is not mankind, but the elect, who are thus related. Christ is not the Brother of the sons of Adam, but of "the seed of Abraham" (HEB. 2:16); for we must take into account not only the nature which He assumed but His intention in assuming it.

Their redemption by Christ adds another peculiarity to the relation of the elect to God. For they, and they only, were redeemed. 1. Because redemption flowed from the electing love of God. "The purpose of God, according to election," defined the people for whom salvation was provided. In behalf of these the Son engaged to act His part, as the Head of the covenant of grace; and for them in fulfilment of His promise, He purchased redemption (JOHN 6:39). And, 2. Because Christ must have been the representative of certain guilty persons, ere satisfaction could be demanded from Him by God, as judge. There could be no sin before the mind of God when He dealt judicially with Christ as surety, unless guilty persons were somehow at His bar. But they could be there only in their representative. The person of the surety was substituted for persons who were guilty. Certain criminals were thus in Him before the view of the Judge; otherwise, no satisfaction could be demanded by Him. This was due by responsible persons who had sinned; and they must have been in the eye of God, ere He could have required or received it on their account.

Being redeemed, His elect are regarded by God as accessible by His Spirit of grace, and as certain of having in the sight of Christ an interest in all the blessings provided by His love. For their sakes the earth is continued, and one generation after another of men is introduced and spared; the gospel is preached to all nations; and the Spirit of God descends and works according to Messiah's promise; that they, being in a state of nature, may pass into a state of grace, and thence at last into a state of glory.

However great the contrast between the destinies of the elect and others, we must not attempt to conceal or lessen the interval which separates them in the view of God. It is a sadly mistaken zeal, for the honour of divine goodness, which moves men to throw in something intermediate, that the chasm may appear less great and impassable. Such attempts reflect on God's way of vindicating His own goodness, and only succeed in obscuring, in the view of men, the sovereignty and riches of His glorious grace.

CHAPTER III.

MAN, AS EVANGELIZED, IN RELATION TO GOD.

THIS NEW RELATION MUST CONSIST WITH THOSE PREVIOUSLY EXISTING—THE PECULIARITY OF THE GOSPEL DISPENSATION—THE FIVE GREAT FACTS OF THE GOSPEL—RELATION OF SINNERS, AS EVANGELIZED, TO GOD, TO CHRIST, TO THE ATONEMENT, TO SALVATION.

IN considering the relation in which men, as evangelized, stand to God, it must not be forgotten,

1. *That it must be consistent with those relations, in which men, as fallen, stand to God*, as these are defined by the terms, and determined by the breach, of the covenant of works. All men are "children of wrath" till they are in Christ. It is as such the gospel addresses them, and such they shall continue, till they "repent and believe the gospel." The mere *revelation* of God's grace cannot alter the relation in which, as sinners, they stand to God, as Judge—a *work* of grace alone can do so. The light of the gospel only makes more manifest how lost they are.

2. *That it must be consistent with "the purpose of God according to election";* for, while I cannot explain how the general proclamation of the gospel consists with the special purpose of God, I must not form any conception of the one which is irreconcilable with the other. There can be no warrant for saying, to all who hear the gospel, that God loves them, nor that Christ is their Head, or their Brother, or their Redeemer; for this would be utterly incompatible with the purposes and arrangements of the Covenant of Grace.

3. *That it is the same as that which was constituted in the days of old, between God and those to whom the covenant was revealed.* In its import and design, the gospel which was preached to Abraham, was the same which is now preached to us (GAL. 3:8). It was then, and it is now, a revelation of the same covenant, the same Messiah, the same love, the same salvation, the same God; and it is designed now, as well as then, for the salvation of God's chosen. The scheme of grace, unfolded under the glimmering light of types, is the self-same on which the full light of the gospel now clearly shines. It could not then have been a scheme of universal benevolence, for it was authoritatively restricted to the circumcised; and it cannot therefore be so now. How, if it were so, could it be consistently administered by its Almighty Author, if providentially restricted, as it still actually is, to a portion of our race?

But though the message of the gospel comes from the same God, reveals the same Messiah, and proposes the same terms of salvation, now as of old, the mode in which it is conveyed is different, and the measure of its light is greater. And, before inquiring how men, to whom the gospel is now preached, stand related to God, we must try to apprehend what the novelty is which gives its distinct character to the evangelic economy, as compared with that which it displaced. This is necessary, because to many minds the change seems as radical as if it were a passing to another covenant, and to another God.

1. *It is not new, because it is Mediatorial.* God's government, bearing on the church, and on all men, had ever been since the fall, through the Son as Mediator. In no other way was a dispensation of grace possible. It was the covenant of which Christ is Head that was administered in Old Testament times. It was He who spake to guilty man in Eden. It was He who appeared to the patriarchs. He was the Angel who led Israel through the wilderness by the hand of Moses (EXOD. 23:20,21). It was He who ordered the equipment of Israel as a nation and a church in the land of promise. It was "the Spirit of Christ" who inspired the prophets (1 PET. 1:11). All the blessings by which the saints of old were enriched, were given in His right and by His Spirit. Then, as well as now, all judgment was in the hands of the Son, as Mediator. But now the Son, as Incarnate, reigns. "The Word made flesh" is now the King of Zion, and the King of nations. The same Person, with the same authority, is on the throne; but He is now seated there, after having been crucified and crowned in the flesh.

2. *The light of Old Testament revelation has not been so eclipsed as to be superseded by the effulgence of the gospel.* True, there is a clearer light now than then. "The last days" have come; and brighter, with light from heaven, there shall not be on earth. "The word of the Lord" which now is "abideth for ever" (1 PET. 1:25). But, if the ancient Scriptures could be of any benefit to the church, would we expect that the "Lord merciful and gracious" would set them aside? Can they not now be all the more instructive than of old? Are they not required for the confirmation of the Christian's faith? Can he embrace the Jesus of the gospels, unless he can recognise Him as the Messiah of the prophets? And the Lord was careful to make it known that it was not His design to supersede the Old Testament Scriptures. At His first teaching after His resurrection, the lesson was taken from Moses and the prophets (LUKE 24:27). He would not allow His disciples to recognise Him in the flesh till they first identified Him with the promised Messiah (LUKE 24:16,31). The sermons preached by His apostles were from Old Testament texts (ACTS 2:16). And when He was inspiring the men who wrote the New Testament, He acknowledged, in countless

instances, the authority of the Old, as still conclusive, in deciding questions both of faith and duty.

3. *The new economy has not arrested the administration of the covenant of Works; nor has it weakened the authority of the moral law to any extent whatever.* All that was typical in the worship of Israel has been superseded; for He, who is "the way, and the truth, and the life," has come. The yoke of the ceremonial law no longer lies on the neck of the church. That "law was a schoolmaster to bring unto Christ" (GAL. 3:24). As a ritual, its design has been fulfilled, and its end has come. But as a part of the revelation, its written rules abide; and through them glimpses of Christ shall be seen, by New Testament saints, to the end of time. And all that was not '*moral*' in the national laws of Israel, is no longer binding on the church. No nation is now a church; no church is now a nation. The Jewish code can no longer be in force; for the covenant according to which it was administered, has decayed, waxed old, and vanished away (HEB. 8:8-13). But there is a law which cannot be set aside; and there is a form of its administration which is still in force—the moral law administered according to the covenant of works. It is the image of God drawn by His own hand. Because He is unchangeable and His work perfect, the moral law can never alter. A clearer light may shine on it than of old, but its features are still the same. And how strange is the delusion of those who imagine, that the gospel, in which appears the highest conceivable proof of God's regard for the honour of His law, and by which is revealed the only possible way of escape from its yoke and its curse, as a covenant, should be regarded as setting it altogether aside, or as intended to teach men to despise it, as if it were utterly invalid or effete. In these three ways, the authority of God must bear on men under the gospel. 1. If unbelievers, they are still under the covenant of works. This is no Jewish peculiarity; it is the natural condition of the children of Adam. 2. If believers, they are "not without law to God, but under law to Christ" (1 COR. 9:21); for no arrangement of their relation to God, can ever remove this essential condition of creatureship. 3. All are bound to submit to the will of God as revealed in the Gospel. They are shut up by divine authority to "the obedience of faith" (ROM. 16:26). But how common is it to ignore these truths; and to regard the gospel as superseding all law, and consulting only the convenience of those who need to be saved.

But the gospel dispensation is *brighter, freer, more catholic,* and *more spiritual* than that which preceded it.

It is *brighter.* "The Word" has been "made flesh" (JOHN 1:14). He has actually "dwelt among" men on the earth, Himself "the Son of man." We have now before us the history of His life of three and thirty years. During that period, what flashes of divine glory shone out of that tabernacle in which He dwelt, making Jesus manifest as "the only Begotten of the Father," to all whose eyes were opened. What light His obedience "unto death" now sheds on the relation of men to the law, and of the law to God; as well as on the divine plan of redemption through the Son. In His dealing with His only Begotten in the flesh, appears the whole character of God; each perfection revealed, and the lustre of all harmoniously blending in His glorious name. He who was crucified and buried is now risen. The work of redemption is actually finished. The blood that made atonement is shed, and accepted, and presented. Jesus has been raised on high; glory has been given to Him, and power, at the right hand of God. His life in the flesh above, with its gracious bearing on the church below, is discovered to the eye of faith. The privileges of believers are fully detailed in the doctrines, and frequently assured in the promises, of the gospel. In the dim light of the apocalypse the future of the visible church appears on to its close, in the awful grandeur of Christ's second coming; and beyond the scene, events and results of the final judgment, are disclosed the eternal glory, bliss, and service of heaven, and the darkness, the woe, and the wailing of hell.

It is *freer*. The removal of cumbrous and costly ceremonies has made it so. Its clearer light, too, secures greater freedom. "The way into the holiest" is now "made manifest" (HEB. 10:19,20). The name of God, who is there, is more clearly made known. There is an opportunity of greater boldness in approaching the mercy-seat. But gospel liberty is not mere escape from burdensome service; it is freedom to serve God with more faith, and love, and reverence. And let it not be forgotten that the gospel dispensation does not secure the liberty of all who are under it. Its being free does not emancipate. Nor are we to think that necessarily New Testament saints have greater liberty of soul than they of old. The Spirit of adoption, as the Spirit of the Son, alone makes free (JOHN 8:36; ROM. 8:15; GAL. 4:6); and, under all the disadvantages of the Old Testament, He enabled some to reach attainments in faith and holiness, which raised them above comparison with many believers of the gospel.

It is *more catholic*. The Mosaic law was a fence as well as a yoke. It formed a "wall of partition" (EPH. 2:14) around the "peculiar people," excluding all the Gentiles, as such, from the society and privileges of the Church of God. But it is now taken down; and the gospel is preached to the Gentiles. "In Christ there is neither Jew nor Greek." This is a new thing; but, since Abraham's day, it might have been expected. The God of Abraham, promised to bless, in Messiah, "all the families of the earth" (GEN. 12:3). When Messiah came "in the fullness

IN RELATION TO GOD.

of time," He was announced to be the "Lamb of God, which taketh away the sins of the world"; and ere He ascended, He commanded the gospel to be preached to all nations (MATT. 28:19). It was thus He appeared to be the Messiah promised to Abraham. If he claims to be "the light of the world," the one "propitiation for the sins of the whole world," the Prince and Saviour to all the nations of the earth, He may thus be recognised as "the hope of Israel" promised to the fathers. The comprehensive reference of New Testament words of hope, accords with the terms of the promise to Abraham. These words of world-wide embrace, were needed in order to the identification of the Christ of God; and that, in their light, the Gentiles might discover that there was hope for them. That Gentile does a foul thing who abuses them as an occasion for misrepresenting the scheme of grace. And yet how many there are who regard the wide words of grace, which they find in the gospel, as intended to teach, that the scheme it unfolds is one of universal love. But it is no new thing to cover a restricted reference in such forms of expression. The promises of grace which were given of old, seemed to embrace all within the area on which the light was shining. "Israel shall be saved in the Lord" (ISA. 45:17) —"Judah shall be saved, and Israel shall dwell safely" (JER. 23:6). These, and many such promises, seemed to embrace all the people to whom the covenant was revealed, although the gracious reference was only to a chosen few. "They were not all Israel" in the sense of the promise, "who were of Israel," as a nation. So now, "all the world," as the gospel area, seems to be embraced in its words of grace; but now, as well as then, there are an elect people, who are the special objects of God's love. All in the world are not "the world" whom God loved "from everlasting," whom He gave to His Son to redeem, and for whom the Son as Surety gave His life a ransom. The design of God, of old, was to gather His chosen out of Israel; His design now, is to gather them out of all nations. *In relation to the area which it illumines, the gracious reference of the gospel is not more universal than that of the revelations of grace given of old to Israel.*

It is *more spiritual.* There is less, for the carnal eye, less for the self-righteous heart, in the simple worship of these gospel days, than in the elaborate ritualism of the days of old. The sun has risen; and all the cumbrous apparatus for giving light by night is now removed. The church is thrown open to the full free light of day. But there are owls that cannot be drawn or driven into the light—there are who will be ritualists still. And how aptly they illustrate their system by their practice! Darkening the windows of their chapels, lest the pure light of day illumine them, they place, upon forbidden altars, candles to give a feebler light. The mosaic law, with its divinely arranged ritual, was once a honeycomb in which Old Testament faith found food and sweetness for the broken heart. But these, loathing the honey, which was expressed from it on Calvary, still cleave to its empty rites. And as not from the honeycomb do they always derive the material for the candles which they use;—for quite as often is it drawn from marshes in which long ages of decay have left their debris;—so quite as much have modern ritualists borrowed from the vile deposits of Pagan superstition, as from the ancient ceremonies of the Jewish church. Ritualism is not mere folly; it is wickedness. It is not merely a thing to be despised as silly; it is a thing to be shunned as deadly. It is not merely like the foolish behaviour of men who amuse themselves with their old nursery toys—who prove their heads to be light, as well as grey, by making sport with the playthings of their earliest youth. It turns into a prison and a slaughter-house the Church of God, where souls are bound with chains, fed with husks, and poisoned with deadly drugs.

And it is more spiritual, not merely because its worship is more simple, but also because it is attended with a more copious and widespread effusion of the Holy Ghost. This followed the ascension of Christ; this marked on earth the youth of His life on high, that the connection might be more evident of the Spirit's procession and work in all ages, with the Person, death, and life of Him who is the Christ of God.

There are five great facts, which demand primary attention from all who would discover the exact relation in which men, as evangelised, stand to God. 1. That the Author of the Gospel is God—that the grace and the message are "of God." 2. That it is "concerning His Son Jesus Christ." 3. That the death of Christ appears prominently in the light of the gospel. 4. That it is about salvation God deals with men by the gospel. And 5. That it is preached to sinners as such.

The Gospel is "of God" (ROM. 1:3). Its message comes to us by Him. We must therefore "give earnest heed." He speaks with divine authority and should be reverenced; He is faithful—"it is impossible for God to lie"—He should therefore be believed. All who hear are bound to attend and believe.

Christ is the great theme of the gospel, the personal Saviour, whom it reveals and presents to us. He is preached as "Jesus Christ the Lord"; His *right* to save, certified by His attested commission and His accepted merit; His *power* to save, extending "to the uttermost" and His *willingness* to save, assured both by His death and by His word. Such is He as presented by God to "every creature under heaven," to whom the gospel is preached.

It is as Christ crucified He is preached (1 COR. 1:23). The gospel requires us to fix special attention on the death of Christ. Its place, in the arrangements of the covenant of grace, requires that it be prominently presented in the light by which that covenant is revealed.

It is to deal with Him about salvation God calls us by the gospel,—about salvation as embodied in His Christ, and as assured to all who by faith receive Him.

And if we ever come it must be as sinners. We cannot exercise faith in Christ, unless we realise that we are sinners; nor will we ever seek an interest in Him. It is not a sense of sin which entitles us to trust in Him. We are required to do so whatever be our state of feeling. As an absolute sinner I *may* trust in Him; but as a whole-hearted sinner I never *will*.

It would be well if preachers of the gospel were more impressed with these great facts. If they preached as men who realised that they carried a message from Jehovah; that the Saviour was the Christ and the Son of God; that His death was the only atonement for sin; that the salvation which is by Jesus Christ, is full, free and everlasting; and that their hearers are sinners ready to perish; how impossible would they then find it to hesitate about requiring faith from all who hear the gospel! No difficulty arising from the sovereignty of God's love, and from the restricted reference of Christ's atonement, could hamper their minds or straiten their feelings in preaching Christ to sinners. All the more free and urgent would they be, as they realised a love, whose purposes must take effect, and a death, that shall not be in vain. And how the light of those great facts would clear men's views of faith, if only they would admit it into their minds! It can be nought else than the reception of the Gospel, as true, because divine, and trust in the Christ of God, whom it reveals as a gracious Saviour from sin.

But we must more minutely consider how sinners, to whom the gospel is preached, are placed in relation to God, to Christ, to the atonement, and to salvation.

1. In thinking of God, as the Author of the gospel, we must not forget that He is the God of the covenant, and that it is by means of the gospel He is fulfilling the purposes and communicating the blessings of that covenant on the earth. His gracious design is to gather His elect to His Messiah, that in Him He may give them grace and glory.

We must remember, too, that the view of God's character given in the light of the gospel must be consistent with former revelations of Himself. He is committed by a threefold exhibition of Himself, which He gave in Old Testament times; and not only must He be consistent with Himself as He then appeared, but there must be in the gospel a fuller and clearer manifestation of Him, in each of these aspects of His character. He appeared as the God of Sinai—Jehovah, the Supreme Ruler, the only Judge, reverend in majesty, glorious in holiness, awful in His wrath. Before Him were a host of cowering slaves, representing our fallen race, dreading His anger, intolerant of His presence, and hopeless of His favour. In relation to these, He appears as the Great "I am," proclaiming His sovereignty, and, by the exercise of His irresponsible will, accounting for His election of some of them as objects of His mercy. According to His everlasting covenant, all is arranged for the fulfilment of His purposes bearing on His chosen; and His name, according to which He is to act in executing His scheme of grace, He declares to be, "Jehovah, Jehovah God, merciful and gracious, long-suffering, and abundant in goodness and truth; keeping mercy for thousands; forgiving iniquity, transgression, and sin; and that will by no means clear the guilty" (EXOD. 34:6,7). This is His character, as it shall be developed in His dealings, in all ages, with men according to His covenant of grace. Thus shall He always express Himself as the God of salvation. His name is no abstraction. It is not something which I can know, while standing at a distance from Himself. He reveals His name in His work; and I can know that name, only when, as a sinner, I transact with Him about salvation. It is only as He acts towards me, according to His name, that I can know Him.

Thus shall God reveal Himself to the end of time—thus is He made known by the gospel. It gives a clearer view of His character, as it was revealed from Sinai; makes a fuller display and furnishes occasion for a continued and more minute assertion of His sovereignty among the nations; and though the glory of His grace appears in the clear light of the doctrines of the cross, it is still as true as ever that none can know, appropriate, or taste His love, but such as have come, because He brought them, to Himself in Christ. The treasures of that glorious name are not sown broadcast over the race of Adam;—He reserves them under His own control. "He will have mercy on Whom He will"; and these as believing sinners lying at His footstool, and only these, shall "taste that the Lord is gracious."

How often and how greatly misrepresented is the character of God, as revealed in the gospel, by those who single out the one attribute of love, and insist on the universality of its regards. To their minds, the view of God, given by the law, seems inconsistent with the love commended in the gospel. The latter they use as an expedient for getting rid of the impressions of God's character, produced by the law. They think they are entitled not to look at the stern aspect of divine glory, as it appears in the lurid light of Sinai. They seem to conceive of an Old Testament God and a New Testament deity altogether different. They cannot honestly say "to us there is one God"; for if they had but one God, how could they reverence Him, unless they recognised Him as one, in all the manifestations of His glory—unless they beheld in the cross the very truth and righteousness which gave so severe an aspect to His character, as revealed from Sinai. It is impossible to respect the God of the gospel unless those views of His character, which gave its distinctiveness to the revelation of old, are seen in a clearer light, and in harmony with His love. It is the glory of the gospel, that in the very measure in which it displays the awfulness of divine wrath, and gives a deeper impression than that given by the law, of the truth and justice of Jehovah, it encourages the sinner to hope for His favour, and to appropriate the gifts of His love. God, as revealed from Sinai, I must not ignore. I must contemplate Him in the light of the law, till my self-righteous hope shall die; and I must recognise Him in the cross, that I may reverence and trust Him.

The gospel of God is *"the gospel of His grace"*—the God of the gospel is "the God of all grace." In its light is seen how "God is love" to Himself and to His people. His Son has been actually given as a Lamb for the sacrifice. All He is, in His divine dignity, and all He is to the Father, as His only Begotten Son, must be considered in thinking of the bounty of the love that gave Him. This gift expressed divine love to sinners—guilty, loathsome enemies. For these the given Son has died, that through His blood they might be reconciled to God; and, as their Head, He has risen, that He might save them by the power of His life.

But this love is *Sovereign*. If God loved, because He was love, and not because He was pleased to love—if the actings of His love were required as an expression of what He was—then its exercise was necessary, and its embrace must be universal. But it is the love of the Almighty, and it must be gratified. It cannot be a fruitless affection. Its purposes must take effect. The final results of His government can furnish no disappointment to His love. It shall have secured at last the perfect blessedness of all whom it embraced. Therefore, the love of God must be sovereign, electing love. And the salvation of the gospel is the provision of love. It is, throughout, a provision suitable, and therefore intended, for sinful persons. The Almighty cannot provide in vain. The benefit He designed must be secured to those for whom it was intended. His love is saving love. He cannot love and not save. Salvation is the necessary expression of His love—this is His one way of making it known. But salvation requires sinful persons as its subjects; therefore love required certain persons as its objects.

Whence springs the anxiety to evade the truth that electing love is the source of all salvation? Let men clothe it as they may, it is the vile progeny of pride. It is the stubborn protest of the carnal mind against the righteousness of the Judge, and against the power of the

Sovereign of all. Men will persist in thinking, that, though sinners, they have some claim on God; or, that, if it is not due to them, God owes it to Himself, to deliver them from death. Oh, that men would only listen to the voice which proclaimeth, "I will have mercy on whom I will have mercy."

There are some who try to imagine an abstract benevolence of Jehovah, different from, and something, as they fain would have it, even higher than, His saving grace, which is discovered through the mediation of His Son. They desire not quite to leave it in the region of the abstract; but they cannot extricate it. They try to think that it may, somehow, find expression in God's general dealings with mankind, by means of the gospel; because they can think of nothing definite. But where, in the firmament of Scripture, does this nebulous thing appear? What is this benevolence, apart from the goodness of God, as Sovereign, which He meantime extends to all, in order to His having an opportunity of fulfilling His purposes of grace? It is one love, and only one, which is revealed in Scripture, the love that gave the Son, and that giveth all things with Him. It is in the outcome of this love that God manifests Himself in Jesus Christ. To some minds it appears as if the manifestation of such love were not after all a revelation of God as love. The direction and expression of His love menwards, originating in a sovereign exercise of His will, seems to them to give occasion for a revelation of His purpose, rather than for an exhibition of Himself. They would therefore introduce a supplementary scheme. They seem to think that God has left room for this. But what is this but to cover a vile impertinence under a cloak of zeal for the honour of God? Let not vain man intrude his suggestions upon God, nor dare to flaunt his anxiety as to the results of divine arrangements, before the eyes of Jehovah. It is by the fulfilment of His purpose, bearing on the elect, God determined to manifest Himself as love—as love to Himself, in the first instance, and to His people in the second. His special purpose only makes Him to appear all the more kingly in His love; and looking to the commendation of His love, which He hath given, it is manifest that He is all He is in loving thus. It is only thus that I could know that "God is love"—that I could recognise Jehovah in the actings of His love, and discern the activity of His love as expressive of all He is.

The love of God was displayed before men, through Jesus Christ; it can affect them only by bringing them to Christ; and it can be expressed to them only when they are in Christ. It was displayed in the gift of the Son, as the Lamb, that through His blood it might flow as saving grace to sinners. It cannot affect them so as to produce any change of state, except through the work of the Holy Ghost in effectual calling. And never, till he is in Christ, can any one be assured of the love of God to him; and never otherwise can the provision, which it hath made, be either obtained or enjoyed.

How prone men are to forget these truths! How strong is the anxiety of unconverted sinners to discover that they are loved already! How many reason thus—'God loved the world; but I am of the world; therefore God loves me.' A most unexceptionable syllogism this, if the premises were true. But in order to determine this, they must follow the world, in the light of Scripture, along the whole line of its revealed connection with the love of God. When they do so, they will discover that the world which the Father loved, He sent His Son to save; that for the life of that world the Son gave His flesh; and that this same world the Spirit convinces "of sin, righteousness, and judgment." They would thus discover that He who can truly say, 'God loves me,' is he, and only he, who has certified his calling by its appropriate fruits, and to whom these have been sealed as evidence of his being in Christ, a son of God, an heir of life eternal. To tell men that God loves them before they have believed, is to tell them what God has not revealed even to His chosen, and what can give no encouragement to a wounded spirit. Such assurance of God's love does not meet the anxious sinner's case. To tell him that God loves him as He hath loved millions who are already in hell, is but to dishearten him, and it dishonours God. This is but to cheat him with "a delusion," and to decoy him with "a snare." His desire is to know how God may express His love to a sinner, and at the same time display His love to Himself. There is no love to which he can lift his eye in hope but free sovereign love, whose exercise consists with all that God is, and with all that God hath said, and whose provision fully and exactly meets such a case as his.

Such views of divine love as have been given raise two questions, which many a fool's attempt has been made to answer.

(1.) Why, if God designed only the salvation of some, does He address the gospel call to all without distinction?

And (2.) How can an earnest call be addressed by God to those whom He doth not love?

(1.) All Calvinists hold that the gracious design of God, in the preaching of the gospel, is the salvation of the elect through faith in Christ; and this is plainly intimated in the Word of God. Why then, it is asked, is the gospel preached to all? The answer must be, that "so it seemed good" in the sight of God; and the arrangement must be accepted as perfect on the credit of God's character. To some extent it may be defended against cavils. *(a.)* It seems *necessary* because the gospel is to be preached by men from whom the "secret things" are hidden. The mysterious thing is not, that the gospel is preached to all, but that it is preached by men. *(b.)* It seems *wise* because it meets the case of God's chosen, as sinners, in a state common to all the race. The gospel of the grace of God is most fitly preached to sinners, as such. From amongst the mass God gathers His chosen by a word and a work of grace adapted to the ruin common to all. He cannot come nigh to these in a revelation of grace without approaching all among whom they are. *(c.)* It is *becoming* that God Himself, and not another, should bring His own loved ones into view, and should do so by a work of grace. *(d.)* There is a design of God, in reference to the non-elect, which shall take effect by means of the gospel, to the praise of His glorious justice. There is a work of judgment, as surely as a work of grace, in connection with the gospel; and however we may shrink from realising this, it is plainly set before us in the light of Scripture (ROM. 11:7-10).

(2.) The difficulty felt by many minds in dealing with the second question, is not owing to the necessary mysteriousness of the divine, but is one of their own creation. Regarding the call of the gospel as necessarily an expression of love, they cannot reconcile it with the doctrine of election. But is the call of the gospel an expression of love to each individual to whom it is addressed? True, the doctrine of the gospel is a revelation of God's love to sinners and the embrace of divine love is assured to all who close with the call of the gospel. But is not this something very different from the call being an expression of love to all to whom it is addressed? True also, the call must be addressed in all sincerity and earnestness by God. But this is secured in perfect consistency with all the doctrines of Calvinism.

Genuine and earnest the gospel call must be, *(a)* because *it presents a claim in behalf of Jesus Christ.* He is infinitely worthy of confidence. He is so in the view of God. His eye rests on the glory of His beloved Son as Jesus Christ when He calls sinners to believe in His name. Till I suspect that God is not in earnest in saying, "this is my beloved Son in whom I am well pleased," I cannot suspect His earnestness in saying "Kiss ye the Son." It must be so, *(b)* because it is a call to accept of Christ as a Saviour in whom the love of God is free, and delights to save all who come to Him. His call to me as a sinner, as it points me to salvation by grace in Christ, is expressive of all the earnestness inspired by God's delight in mercy. It must be so also *(c)* because salvation by grace is to the praise of His glory. This is the terminus to which He calls the sinner. His call is therefore expressive of all the earnestness of His zeal for His own glory. And it must be so *(d)* as a call to believe, because once it has pleased God to testify regarding Jesus Christ, it cannot be a matter of indifference to Him whether men believe or not. His zeal for the claims of His own truth, and for the honour of His name as the God of truth, pours an infinite tide of earnestness into "the word of faith."

It is to divine earnestness, as thus accounted for, our minds should be directed when we are plied with gospel calls. The Son and His worthiness; salvation by grace to the glory of God; the truth and the authority of God;—these should be considered as accounting for the genuineness and earnestness of the calls addressed to us. When a sinner is in earnest under the power of the gospel, it is because these elements of the divine earnestness have touched his heart through faith. The gospel as the testimony of God, as an authoritative assertion of the Son's claims, and as revealing a peace in the hand of mercy, bright with the lustre of God's glorious name, has set his soul in motion in unison with the mind of God. Divine earnestness, thus expressed in the gospel, has been borne in upon his soul, and its strong current bears him on to Christ.

Especial care should ever be taken *not to dissociate God's love from Christ*. There must be zeal for the *holiness* as well as for the *freeness* of the love of God. But to tell a sinner that God loves him apart from Christ, is to represent the love of God so as to provoke contempt—as a love adapting itself to the sinners convenience, rather than as a love which God becomingly expresses. How can the love of God be fitly expressed but in providing Christ as a Saviour, in bringing sinners unto Him, and in blessing them with all spiritual blessings in Him when they come?

In perfect harmony, with all God is, and with all His antecedents and utterances, a sinner may be told that he is a child of disobedience and of wrath, under the yoke and curse of the broken covenant, but that God has provided a Saviour for such sinners as he (ACTS 2:22-36); that, in that Saviour God is willing to show the riches of His grace, in justifying, adopting, and sanctifying all who receive Him; that it shall be to the praise of His glory thus to bless them and that all, who hear the gospel, are required by God, to believe in Christ, in order that the promise of salvation may be theirs in Him. What is there in such a declaration awanting in order to its being a word of hope to sinners, or to forbid its being preached in the name of God? It presents a salvation sure and free in a Saviour provided by God, resulting in glory to God in the highest. It exhibits the love of God as a holy and a saving love. It allows to the sinner no legitimate alternative but faith. God's word of authority shuts him up to God's love in Christ in whom salvation, full, free, and everlasting, is assured to every believer by the counsel and oath of Him for whom it is impossible to lie.

2. "The gospel of God" is *"concerning His Son Jesus Christ."* The

Person, who is the Christ and the Son of God, is presented to us in the gospel. It is a personal Saviour—a saving Person—the gospel reveals to us. He Himself must be realised, received, and trusted. True, it is by faith. It is as exhibited in the truth, He is to be known; and it is by faith in the truth He is to be received. The soul's act of trust cannot immediately reach the person of Christ. It is through the truth alone He is approached. But it is the part of God to see to it, that in connection with the act of faith, there is a vital union formed between the person of the believer and the Person of Christ. It must be so; for I cannot be "in Christ," so as to be regarded by God as standing in His right as Surety, unless I am in Christ, as a member is in union with the Head, or as its living branch is in union with the vine,—so "joined to the Lord" as to be "one spirit with Him." And there can be no exercise of living faith unless the living Christ is realised. It is in Him I must trust. I must be persuaded that He can save me. I require not merely a promise from God assuring me of salvation; I must, in the light of His doctrine, recognise in the flesh Jesus as the Christ and the Son of God (JOHN 6:69). An assurance of salvation by promise would not satisfy me, unless I so knew Him in whom that promise is given, as to be assured that He was worthy of my confidence.

How vain is all faith that reaches not the living Christ of God! And does not that faith stop short of Him which merely grasps a statement regarding the love of God or the death of Christ, and on that warrant appropriates the promise of salvation? There are whose faith is a mere assent to the statements that God loves, and that Christ died for, sinners. These have but the swaddling-clothes—they find not the "child born" and the "Son given." They have the grave-clothes instead of the risen Christ Himself. How much passes, in these days of child's play with the work of God, under the name of conversion, that terminates in no more fruitful result. The gospel is perverted to suit the sinner's convenience, that he may have the joy of hope and the fervour of feeling which this excites, while Christ Himself is ignored, and the soul unrenewed remains apart from Him, and far off from His God.

But there is another snare for anxious souls laid by the tempter's hand. They may be urged to attempt to lay hold of Christ apart from the truth, when they discover the error of taking hold of the truth apart from Christ. A picture of Christ in their imagination, is substituted for Christ as revealed in the word, and to this self-created thing they direct their hope. This is just as fatal a mistake as the other. To sever "what the Lord hath joined" is in either case a deadly blunder. The truth revealing Christ is the only warrant of faith; Christ, as revealed in the truth, is the only object of faith. I can reach Christ

IN RELATION TO GOD.

only by means of the word; and I find nothing there if I reach not Christ Himself.

And it is Christ, *as a Saviour,* who is preached to me in the gospel. He is the only one invested with that office by God. He is the Saviour of the *elect,* and therefore the Saviour of *sinners.* It is as the Saviour of sinners He is presented to me. He is not *officially* or *designedly* the Saviour of the world; but He is engaged to be the Saviour of every sinner who believes. He holds Himself in readiness to save every sinner who comes to Him at the call of God (JOHN 6:37,40).

3. It is "Christ crucified" that is preached in the gospel. His death stands out prominently in gospel light. This is the outstanding fact connected with the name of Christ. This is fitting, because of the place which His atoning death occupies in the scheme of redemption, and its bearing on the glory of God, and on the salvation of His people. In His death He finished a work by which God's justice was satisfied, His law magnified, and His name glorified on earth. By His death He sealed the everlasting covenant of grace, and procured a right to all its blessings for those whom the Father gave Him. It is on the ground of the work finished on the cross, and on that ground alone, that a sinner can attain in Christ, a right to salvation. This is all I can find even in Him on which to rest my hope of peace, and to claim a right to everlasting life.

The place which His death occupies in the gospel, and its important bearing on the destinies of men, tends to induce special attention to our relation to the atonement, and to beget a desire to enjoy the hope of an interest in it. There is in every soul, in whom conscience is active, a feeling of insecurity. There is, in every mind, containing any acquaintance with gospel truth, the idea that an interest in Christ's death is essential to safety. There is in every unrenewed heart a desire to avoid the necessity of dealing with a personal Saviour, and to attain to hope, through the gospel, without being "born again." The figment of a universal atonement, has been produced to meet this craving. It is just the gospel perverted to suit the taste of proud carnal man. 'Christ died for all, and therefore for me; I believe this, and therefore I shall be saved,' are the short stages of an easy journey to the hope of peace. But there is a triple error here—the personal reference is separated from the gracious design of the death of Christ; the death is dissociated from the person of Christ; and the work of the Holy Ghost is ignored.

[1.] *The personal reference is separated from the gracious design of the death of Christ.* If Christ died, He died as a surety. If He died as surety He must have been substituted for those for whom He died. If He died as their substitute, He died so that they all died in Him. Their death is past in His for them (2 COR. 5:14). He died that they might live. This was the design of Christ in reference to those for whom He died. This design must have been in His view, in connection with all who were represented by Him. But to say that there are for whom Christ died, who shall themselves die for ever, is to separate the reference from the design of His death, and to presume to know the purpose of God in another way than that in which alone He is pleased to discover it; for surely it is only as the gracious design takes effect that the personal reference can possibly be made known. It is along the line of divine intention the current of saving grace flows forth to men through Jesus Christ. It is along the wire that the electric current passes through the ocean; but the wire must be hid ere it can conduct the subtle stream. It must be carefully covered, and all the wrapping which conceals it, must extend to the further shore. The current is stopped when the covering is pierced. It is when the section of the whole cable has reached, that the message can be carried to, the further shore; and only then can the wire be denuded and exposed to view. Thus is the chain of love from heaven to earth covered with the design of salvation to sinners. It is when the saving benefit of Christ's death has reached a sinner, that the reference is discovered to him; and then only can the hand of faith grasp the love itself, from which all salvation flows.

To attempt to determine the reference, so as to ascertain the parties for whom Christ died, till this is discovered by the application of redemption, and to use that supposed reference as a rule of faith, is to pry presumptuously into divine secrets, and to substitute the decretive for the revealed will of God. This error, so often charged against Calvinists, is committed rather by those who charge them with it.

[2.] *The death is dissociated from the person of Christ.* To believe that Christ died for me, because He died for all, is to "believe a lie"; but even were it true, of what advantage could this faith be of to me? His dying for me, because for all, secures nothing to me. And to believe this, is something else than to believe in Christ Himself. It is in effect, making His death a substitute for Himself. But instead of looking on the death of Christ as it refers to you, look, in the first instance, on its bearing on His own fitness to save, and on the prospects of all who are one with Him. To view it thus, is to see Christ commended instead of superseded by His death. The first thing, I require to be assured of, is Christ's fitness to save me, a sinner. It is in Him I am called to trust. Ere I can do so, I must be persuaded that He is worthy of my confidence. This I cannot be assured of, unless I know Him as a sacrifice for sin (HEB. 9:14). The merit of His sacrifice I cannot appreciate, but in the light of His personal glory; and I cannot appropriate the benefits secured by it, till I have first taken hold of Himself by faith (EPH. 1:7). What I discover in the light of the cross is, that He can save me in a way that shall be to the glory of God. This is His grand recommendation as a Saviour to me. If this were not true regarding Him, I never could confide in Him. And in the light in which I realise the infinite merit of His sacrifice, I know His love to be such as "passeth knowledge." To connect that love, and the death by which it was commended, with those whom the Father gave to Him, does not deprive me of hope. It only assures me of how certain, and therefore how desirable the redemption is, which was purchased by His blood. The Person, in all His power and love, is presented to me; and the authority of God shuts me up to the acceptance of Him, in order to my own salvation. It is light revealing the glorious person, the infinite merit, and the ineffable love of Christ, and a call requiring me to come to Him, and not any supposed reference of His death to me, that encourages me to receive Him that I may be saved.

[3.] *The Spirit's work is practically ignored.* There is nothing in the exercise of an Arminian's faith opposed to the tendencies of man unrenewed. A sense of danger is excited in his breast by a guilty conscience. His very selfishness inclines him to grasp some object of hope. He cannot expect to be safe apart from the hope of the Gospel. But the carnal mind recoils from dealing with a divine person, and the pride of the old heart rebels against being the subject of a work of grace. Thence arises the desire for a hope, that seems connected with the gospel, while ignoring the person of Christ and the work of the Holy Ghost. A recognition of the Spirit's work cannot find a place in such a system, and that work is not required in order to the production of such a faith.

There are some who, Calvinists in their vows and Arminians in their tendencies, teach the doctrine of a double reference of the atonement; representing the atonement as offered in one sense for the elect, and in another sense for all. These maintain that there was a special atonement securing a certainty of salvation to some, and a universal atonement securing a possibility of salvation to all.

Subscribers of the Confession of Faith, who advocate the double reference of the atonement, profess to believe that Christ died in a sense for the elect, in which He died for none besides—that He died because He was their surety—that their sins alone were imputed to Him—that it is His relation to the elect which accounts for His death—that for them alone redemption was purchased—and that to none besides shall redemption be applied. How can they then consistently hold that Christ died for all? There are two ways in which a reconciliation of the two references may be attempted:—[1.] It may be said that the call of the gospel must involve the salvability of those to whom it is addressed. This is traced to the death of Christ as an atonement of infinite value; and on that ground and to that effect it may be insisted that Christ died for all. But how can this consist with this other doctrine, which they profess to believe—that no one is salvable without atonement. No atonement can make my salvation possible if it did not satisfy divine justice for my sins.

How can the possibility of my salvation be before the mind of God, unless He sees my sins atoned for in the death of Christ? How could they be atoned for unless they were imputed to Him? And how could they be imputed to Him unless He was my surety? Thus, and thus alone, could He make possible the salvation of any. If it be objected, that unless the salvation of all who are called is possible there is no hope for them, it is enough to reply, that just as surely as salvation is not possible without atonement, neither is it so without faith; and that instead of tracing the possibility of a universal salvation to a universal reference of the atonement, the wise and the right thing would be, to insist on the ability of Christ to save all who come to Him; on the certainty of salvation through faith; and on the impossibility of salvation without it. But this universal reference, of which so much is made, is after all no reference of the atonement.

There is no atonement that does not imply satisfaction to divine justice. There was no satisfaction of justice that did not avail to the purchase of redemption. Is there a universal reference of such an atonement to all? If not, of what atonement? And if of another, how can it avail to make salvation possible? To say that the atonement, being of infinite value, is sufficient for all, is beside the mark, for the question is as to the divine intention. To say, that, if the atonement was of infinite value, it was intended to be so, is to rhapsodise considerably: for, surely, the value of the atonement does not flow from the intention of God the Father, but from the dignity of God the Son, who offered it.

[2.] It may be said, that there are many mercies, of which all partake, which they owe to the death of Christ, and that, to this effect, He may be said to have died for all,—that He died to procure some good for all, as well as to procure all good for some. It is quite true, that, because of the purpose of God bearing on the elect, many mercies are bestowed on others; and that it is the death of Christ which has secured the honourable fulfilment of that purpose. But this is the only connection between the good, given to all, and the death of Christ. It is merely an accident of the process by which all good is conveyed to some. Christ hath "power over all flesh," but this was given to Him "that He might give eternal life to as many as the Father gave Him." This power He hath in reward of His death, but He hath it for the salvation of His chosen. He died to procure all good for them; and if, in the exercise of His Sovereign power, He showers some good on all, He does it with a view to the preservation of our race, and to its development in successive generations, till He shall have gathered His chosen out of it.

The doctrine of the double reference is an oil and water mixture;—it is opposed to Scripture;—no one who has subscribed the Confession of Faith can consistently hold it;—it adopts the practical bearing of Arminianism;—it endangers the doctrine of the atonement,—and it is quite unavailing for the purpose to which it is applied.

[1.] Those who hold it are in a transition state, and occupy no fixed dogmatic ground. Sometimes they seem staunch Calvinists, and at other times utter Arminians. They try to move on the boundary line between the two systems, and would fain keep a foot on either side. But the fence is too high to admit of this. They therefore display their agility in leaps from side to side. But this is very fatiguing work, and must soon be given up. They will find that they must walk on either side. As it was an Arminian bias that moved them to these gambols, the most probable finale is, that they shall utterly abandon the Calvinistic side.

[2.] It is opposed to Scripture. As seen in Bible light, the death of Christ is indissolubly connected with *(a)* the covenant love of God, of which it was the gift that it might be the channel; *(b)* with imputed sin as its procuring cause; and *(c)* with redemption as its infallible result (JOHN 3:16; ROM. 5:8; 2 COR. 5:21; ROM. 8:32). To insist on a reference of the death of Christ to any who were not loved by God, whose sins were not imputed to, and atoned for by Christ, and who shall not be saved, is therefore utterly opposed to Scripture. The way to conceal the manifest unscripturalness of this position is, to raise the dust of a double reference around it, by saying that it is not in the same sense Christ died for the elect, as for others. The special reference is not denied; it is so plainly taught in Scripture. But where in Scripture is the other? A reference to 1 JOHN 2:2 has been given as an answer to this question. But if there is a passage more conclusive than any other against the doctrine of a double reference it is that very one. It plainly teaches that in the self-same sense in which Christ is the propitiation for the sins of those whose cause He pleads as Advocate, He is so "for the sins of the whole world"—of all to whom His atonement refers. In all those passages, which seem to some to teach the doctrine of a universal reference of the death of Christ, it is seen connected either with love, or suretyship, or redemption, and if with either, it cannot possibly be a death for all. Calvinistic Universalists are challenged to produce a passage from the Word of God which seems to support their view, not containing in itself, or in its context, one of these limitations.

[3.] No subscriber of the Confession can both intelligently and honestly maintain the doctrine of the double reference of the atonement. It is not in the Confession; it is inconsistent with several of its statements; and a view of the question as to the reference of the atonement was present to the minds of the Westminster divines, utterly incompatible with any such doctrine.

The doctrine of 'the double reference' is not in the Confession of Faith. The only attempts made to find it there have resulted in utter failure. All that can be said by its advocates is, that there is one sentence in the Confession, with which it is not inconsistent. That sentence is, "The Lord Jesus, by His perfect obedience and sacrifice of Himself, which He, through the Eternal Spirit, once offered up unto God, hath fully satisfied the justice of the Father." All that can be maintained is, that the new doctrine does not contradict that statement, because it indicates no reference at all, and connects no result with the satisfaction of justice. But why did Christ require to satisfy the justice of the Father? Was it not because sin was charged to His account? And why was He thus chargeable, but because He was "the Just for the unjust?" The idea of Christ satisfying justice, except as the Surety of His people, and to the effect of purchasing redemption for them, is utterly opposed to the whole teaching of the Confession, and cannot therefore be in the passage quoted. And why are these words dissevered from what follows? Are not the obedience and sacrifice of Christ declared to avail, not merely for satisfaction, but for purchasing, "not only reconciliation, but an eternal inheritance in the kingdom of heaven for all those whom the Father hath given unto Him?" His work, finished on the cross, had all this efficacy in it for behoof of those for whom He died. To maintain that it availed to a certain extent for all, and to the full extent for some, is a doctrine utterly unwarranted by the passage referred to. If Christ died, He died with that whole design; and to that full effect He died for them, for whom He died at all.

But the doctrine of the double reference is utterly opposed to some statements of the Confession of Faith. The doctrine of the Confession is, that Christ is "the Mediator and Surety" in order to redeem, call, justify, sanctify, and glorify a people whom the Father gave Him from all eternity; that in order "that He might discharge" that office; "he was made under the law," and did perfectly fulfil it; was crucified and died; that "Christ by His obedience and death, did fully discharge the debt of all who are justified, and did make a proper, real, and full satisfaction to his Father's justice in their behalf." In all these passages, the mediation of Christ, in its design, in the reference of its fundamental act, and in its gracious results, is restricted to the elect. What Westminster divine would say, Christ died for "the rest of mankind" whom "God was pleased, according to the unsearchable counsel of His own will, whereby He extendeth or withholdeth mercy as He pleaseth, for the glory of His sovereign power over His creatures, to pass by, and to ordain them to dishonour and wrath for their sin, to the praise of His glorious justice"?

There was a view of the question before the minds of the Westminster divines utterly incompatible with the doctrine of the double reference. The statements in the Confession, bearing on the atonement, were adapted to the state of the question of the extent of the atonement, as discussed between Calvinists and the French Universalists. Both parties held, *that Christ redeemed all for whom He died,* and neither therefore could hold the double reference. The difference between them is indicated in the words, "To all those for whom Christ hath purchased redemption, he doth certainly and effectually communicate the same." The difference between the views of the French Universalists and the doctrine of the double reference is, that according to the former, Christ died for all indiscriminately, and did by His death redeem them; while according to the latter, election determined a special reference of the atonement to the elect, in order to their redemption, but not excluding a reference to all, in order to something not very easily defined.

[4.] It adopts the practical bearing of Arminianism. It must have been originally invented by some weak Calvinist, who thought that the Arminian had an advantage which he lacked, in plying sinners with the gospel call. The suasion of universal grace seemed, in his view, to give the other an immense practical power. He therefore stole from him as much as would place him on an equal footing, in the practical use of doctrine. He remained, *ex professo,* a Calvinist, that he might keep hold of his creed, and became, *de facto,* an Arminian, that he might get hold of his hearers. And there are preachers not a few, who seem to think that, though their speculations must be conformed to the system of Calvinism, as the only scientific arrangement of "the things of God," they must be Arminians when they deal with the consciences of sinners. The consequence is, that so far as a practical presentation of doctrine is concerned, they are Arminians if they are anything. To tell men that Christ died for all, and that this is the basis on which the call to all is founded, is to quit hold of all that is distinctive in Calvinism in order to command the sympathies of a heart unrenewed. By such a form of doctrine many teach more than they intend. Its phrases suggest to many minds the idea of universal grace, and encourage them in a Christless hope. Any protest against universal grace which may be mingled with such utterances can be easily separated. The two elements are so incongruous that they will not combine; and in the hands of unconverted men it is not difficult to tell which shall be removed.

[5.] It endangers the whole doctrine of the atonement. It is impossible to account satisfactorily for the death of Christ, except by ascribing it to His bearing imputed sin, with a view to His making atonement for it. It is impossible to account for His being "made sin," but by His substitution for a guilty people. But if men believe that Christ died for many whose sin He did not bear, whose surety He was not, and whose redemption he did not purchase, they are adrift on a current which may carry them down to Socinianism. An Arminian, with his single universal reference, may in a vague indefinite form hold by the doctrine of substitution, as he thinks of Christ as the representative of mankind, and may have some steadfast idea of atonement for sin in his mind. But believers in a double reference can have no clear view, and no firm hold of the doctrine of substitution at all. They are more in danger therefore of moving towards Socinianism than even the undisguised Arminian. Generations may pass before that tendency is fully developed in ecclesiastical formulas, but the dangerous tendency is there, and the sooner it is eliminated the better.

[6.] It is quite unavailing for the purpose to which it is applied. It, doubtless, sprung out of a desire to find a basis for the offer of Christ to all. To search for it, in a universal reference of the atonement, indicated a suspicion that the Calvinistic system did not afford it. What helpless ignorance such a suspicion indicates! How sad it is to hear men, sworn to Calvinism, declare that without this theft from the Arminian stores they could not preach the gospel at all! Do they believe that "Christ is all in all"; that God's testimony regarding Him is true; and that they are commanded to preach "the gospel of God concerning His Son Jesus Christ" to every creature? If so, what can they desiderate in order that they may say to every sinner to whom they preach "Believe on the Lord Jesus Christ and thou shalt be saved?" This is the Scripture version of the gospel call; and I can never hesitate to proclaim it till I conclude that Christ is unworthy of being trusted, and God unworthy of being believed. The idea of the call being the offer of a gift has driven the scriptural form of it out of the minds of many men altogether. This other was the form it alone assumed in the thinking and teaching of "the Marrow-men." To their successors it suggested more than these fathers meant. They began to regard it as necessarily an expression of love to the individual to whom it is addressed. They desiderated some sort of interest of all in

Christ before the call is accepted, in order to justify its being given. Extending the idea of the Marrow-men's "deed of gift and grant," they reached at last the universal reference of the atonement, while still stretching a long arm to keep a weak hold of the Calvinism of the Confession. They hesitate not to say that without the universal reference they could not preach the gospel at all—in other words, that this is the only basis they find for the call of the gospel. And what do they find there on which to base the offer? A reference that avails for no definite end; that secures no redemption; and that leaves those whom it connects with the death of Christ to perish in their sins. This and no more they find; and on this they base the offer of the gospel!

Verily, if men cannot preach the gospel without this, it is difficult to see how this can help them. There is some carnal sense in the Arminian view, but this lacks even that. If Christ died to redeem all men, there seems something like a basis for a call to believe in Him to the saving of the soul. But this reference, outside of that which election is held to have defined, and which connects the chosen exclusively with redemption, is a palpably unsatisfactory thing. Does it even avail to secure an offer of salvation to all? No one can say it does, when millions have perished, and there are millions still on earth, who never heard the gospel. To what effect then does it avail? To secure the extension to all of God's providential goodness. And on what avails only to that extent the offer of salvation is based! What to me, an immortal and sinful soul, on the brink of Eternity, is a message telling me that "bread which perisheth" was procured for me by the death of Christ! It is salvation I require—it is for that I agonise. I care not for vague references. Give me a living Saviour, to whom I may commit my soul; give me a "sure word of prophecy" regarding Him; give me a divine command to believe in His name. Then and thus, and only then and thus, can my wearied soul find aught to lean on; and I shall count it both my privilege and my duty, to yield my homage to divine authority, my faith to divine testimony, and my trust to a divine Redeemer.

4. In thinking of the salvation revealed in the gospel, there are two extremes, between which the Spirit of God alone can guide us. It must not be regarded, either as something so reserved for the elect, as to preclude the offer of it by God to sinners, as such; or as something which any sinner can claim, as intended for him, and because it meets his case. It is possible to look on salvation exclusively in its relation to God and to the covenant; and while careful not to cherish such views of it as remove it from divine control, and ignore its bearing on the divine glory, to neglect its relation to men and its adaptation to their state as sinners. And it is also possible so to conceive of

it, in its relation to man, as suitable to his case and near to his hand, as to ignore its connection with the covenant of grace, and its bearing on the glory of the name of God. From both these extremes our minds would be preserved, if we viewed salvation *as embodied in the Christ whom the gospel reveals, and as embosomed in the promise given, to all who believe in His name.* To me, a sinner, to whom the gospel is preached, Christ Himself is presented, as the "wisdom, righteousness, sanctification, and redemption," which make up "the great salvation" of the Lord. I cannot appropriate that salvation but by the hand that has grasped "the Christ of God" Himself. As I look to Him with the eye of faith, how suitable, how gracious, how holy, how perfect, how divine seems the salvation which is brought nigh to me. If I at all appreciate it I would fain enjoy it. But I must not try to conceive of it as in some sense mine before I have believed. As embosomed in the promise, it belongs only to them that believe.

The doctrine that God has in the Gospel published, "a deed of gift and grant" constituting Christ, in some sense, the property of all to whom "the word of salvation" is sent, might in some minds be no deadly poison, and might in some hands do no deadly work, because regarded and explained as meaning, that Christ might warrantably be received by faith; but it has dangerous tendencies. It ministers to the prevalent craving for a hope, not resulting from actual faith in the living Christ of God.

Our relation to the salvation of the gospel is such, that it cannot be ours till we are in Christ through faith; that we are required by God to accept of it in Him; and that it shall infallibly be ours if we believe in His name.

The views which have been presented of the relation in which men, as evangelized, stand to God, to Christ, to the atonement, and to salvation, accord with the doctrine of the model gospel sermon furnished by Christ Himself (JOHN 6). It was addressed to a mixed audience, but was specially directed to those who proved themselves to be unbelievers.

In that sermon sinners are urged to seek, as "the one thing needful," everlasting life (v.27).

Divine authority is asserted by a claim to faith from all who hear the gospel (v.29).

Divine love is exhibited as commended in the gift of the Son to be "the Bread of Life" (v.32); but it is sovereign electing love (v.39).

Christ Himself is presented as "the bread of life" (v.35).

His atoning death is exhibited in connection with His Person, as securing His fitness to be "the Bread of life" to sinners, and as purchasing everlasting life for all for whom it was endured (v.51).

IN RELATION TO GOD.

All that is said, both of God and of His Christ, tends to shut men up in utter helplessness to the grace of the Holy Ghost; and sinners are as plainly told that they cannot come, unless the Father draws them, as that they may come, because the Father calls them (v.44).

By this, and not by the Epistles, which are addressed to believers; by this, and not by the Sermon on the Mount, which is just a practical exposition of the law of Christ, all sermons to mixed audiences should be tried. How much that goes by the name of evangelical preaching is found to be utterly reprobate when subjected to this test. To a mixed audience Christ preaches the doctrine of election, and makes a practical use of it in shutting men up to the Sovereign authority and love of the Father, as representative of the Godhead. How different from this is the practice of those preachers, who 'fly as pestilential' all reference to election, and who eschew those views of God's character and salvation, and of men's spiritual condition, which prove faith to be impossible to a soul unrenewed.

CHAPTER IV

MAN, AS IN CHRIST, IN RELATION TO GOD.

THE RELATION THREEFOLD—REGENERATION—RELATION OF THE REGENERATED TO THE SPIRIT, TO THE SON, TO THE FATHER—JUSTIFICATION—AN ACT BY GOD THE JUDGE—A BLESSING FROM GOD THE SOVEREIGN—ITS OBJECT, GROUND, ELEMENTS, AND EFFECTS—ADOPTION, ITS PLACE, ITS OBJECT, ITS EFFECT—DOES IT CONSTITUTE A SONSHIP IDENTICAL WITH CHRIST'S?

ALL who are in Christ are born again, are "justified freely by grace," and are "the children of God by faith in Christ Jesus." There are thus three lines along which we must trace their relation to God.

I. They are "born again." Once they were "dead in trespasses and sins"; their souls being then of spiritual life as void as is of soul that body which lies putrid in the grave (EPH. 2:4,5). But in the right of Christ, their federal Head, who, with His blood did seal the covenant of grace, and is therefore entitled to apply its provision to His redeemed, the Holy Spirit quickened them. In doing so He expressed His own divine and sovereign love (JOHN 15:26); but, according to the scheme of redemption, He came from the Father as the representative of the Godhead, to fulfil His purpose, and from Christ, who, as exalted Mediator, hath power to send Him, that He may see his promised seed (JOHN 16:7).

The life which the Spirit communicated is distinct, though inseparable, from Himself (EZEK. 36:26,27). It is the life of God—a principle kindred to what God is in His moral character; a holy thing which cannot sin; a seed which cannot die. This principle of spiritual life is in the soul as one essence. The soul thus quickened has a new tendency in all its faculties, and a new power to be developed in all its modes of action. Regeneration has introduced a germ of all holiness—a "new man," complete in all his members. All the graces of the Spirit are seminally in this principle, though there is an order in their development, and though each phase of the spiritual life has its own distinctive character. "Faith" must be its first development in the soul of an adult; "hope and charity" are inseparable from it, but in its train; and though it is one principle that is developed in these, faith is not hope, nor is hope charity. They differ as modes of action, though they express the same principle.

This regeneration results in a new birth—the former being the work of the Spirit, the latter, the change through which the subject of that work passes (JOHN 3:3). This new birth is the soul's entrance, through union to Christ, within the bonds of the covenant of grace. Christ, who magnified the law as a covenant of works, and thus redeemed His people from its curse and yoke, has a right to come to them by His Spirit, as they lie under it, to bring them living out of bondage. Their union to the Adam, in whom they sinned and died, is lawfully and actually dissolved, and they are now in the Second Adam, in whom they are righteous and shall live for ever. In the case of an adult it cannot be said that the new birth is complete without faith. There can be union to Christ without it, for an infant can be born again; but no unbelieving adult can enter the Kingdom of God (JOHN 3:36; 1:12,13). Regeneration precedes and produces faith; but the exercise of that faith is necessary in order to the change implied in the new birth of an adult.

In the person thus quickened and in Christ, the Holy Spirit dwells (1 COR. 6:19; 2 COR. 6:16). The "body"—the whole person—is the tabernacle of His presence, but the new heart is the special place of His rest. And "he who is joined to the Lord is one spirit with Him"; for the Spirit who, in all His fulness, dwells in Christ the Head, dwells also in him the member, in order to preserve from destroyers the holy place of His gracious presence, and to sanctify the whole temple unto God.

The regenerated are therefore subjects of the work, and temples of the presence, of the Holy Ghost; they are the seed and the members of Christ the Son; and they are of, and in, God the Father.

1. The Spirit dwells and works within them. He hath wrought upon them as the Quickener, and He shall work within them as the Sanctifier (GAL. 5:25). And He must "abide with" them. His presence is essential to the continuance of life. All life is of Him, and by Him only can it be preserved. Our bodies live because they live in Him. All the more must there be a special nearness of the Spirit to the spiritual life—a special dependence of it on Him, and a special presence of Him with it. It is in Him, too, our bodies "move" as well as "live." All the more also must there be a special operation of His power, in order to any of all the movements of the spiritual life.

In that same soul, wherein are the life and the presence of God, there is a body of death and the presence of Satan. There is in that soul an army with which Satan may be present, and to which he brings up reserves from hell; and yet the seed of God and the Spirit of God are there. There are "the companies of two armies" in this "Shunamite"; and they are engaged in conflict. "The flesh lusteth against the spirit, and the spirit against the flesh" (GAL. 5:17); and through these the power of God and the power of Satan come into collision in the quickened soul.

At first sight, this arrangement seems irreconcilable with the divine character, an incorrect expression of the divine love, and an inadequate triumph of the divine power. But a closer examination will, to some extent, discover, that it is really glorifying to God, gracious to the saint, and mortifying to Satan.

To God it is glorifying. This way of approaching the object of His love exhibits the glory of His condescension. The Higher He, and the more lowly the loved one, and the more intimate His nearness to the quickened soul, the more manifest shall this appear. And thus to display His kindness quite becomes His holiness. He has created a holy place for Himself within that soul. Through the new heart alone He comes into contact with that soul, and through that holy thing alone His power pulses through the temple of His presence. He works there, to destroy sin—by a baptism of fire to consume it utterly away. His power, even in that secret place where its working is so hidden, shall prove itself omnipotent to save. And His abiding and still working there, in the face of countless provocations, till the subject of His grace is ready for "the presence of His glory" shall demonstrate His unchanging truth and faithfulness.

To the Saint it is gracious. The Holy Spirit came to him unsought, when he was at his worst. He took up His abode within his soul, though all sin was still present there. He carries on His work in the face of many provocations of His holy anger. This is surely a display of love in the Person of the Holy Ghost, for which His saints shall give Him praise for ever. How much matter for eternal song shall they gather from their experience of abounding sin, and of grace much more abounding, during all their life, as temples of the Holy Ghost on earth!

To Satan it is mortifying. There, in the depths of a soul in whom he wrought and reigned before, he meets the presence and the power of God. He met the Godhead in the flesh before, but that flesh was sinless, and it subsisted in the Person of the Son of God. But here into the palace where he himself reigned before, the Holy Ghost hath entered. All sin is still there, and Satan is allowed to work through it against the life and the power of God. But the work of grace makes progress. The power that issues from "the inner man" triumphs over all the wiles and efforts of the enemy, till at last no trace of his presence, and no scar from the conflict shall appear on the soul of the saint. Satan's assaults, with all else, shall have only worked for good to him, who is "the temple of the Holy Ghost."

2. They are the seed and the members of Christ. As Mediator He is their Head. As such He transacted in their behalf with God in the

everlasting covenant. All the provision of grace, which is "of God" according to that covenant, dwells in Him. Originally "all things are of God" (2 COR. 5:18). If Christ is "the Head of every man," "the Head of Christ is God" (1 COR. 11:3). But in mediatorial relation to His people, Christ is Head. As their Federal Head they were so in Him, that, as to their spiritual being and wellbeing, He is their "everlasting Father" (ISA. 9:6). They were in Him in the days of His flesh. He bore them, hidden in Himself, through all His work, His sorrow, His dying, and His resurrection—He wrought and suffered with a view to their being born again of Him by His Spirit into a state of grace. Their life comes from His travail. They, as living souls, are His seed. He by his travail secured a right to life for them, and opened up a way by which the Spirit of life might come to quicken them. By the Spirit's power they were brought alive, and brought to Christ, that He might "see His seed," and, enjoying them as "the fruit of the travail of His soul," be "satisfied."

Being thus His seed, they must be His *members*. They must be so in order to the communication of covenant grace to them. In Him all its fullness dwells. Apart from Him they cannot receive out of it "grace for grace." Their wants cannot be supplied, unless they are in living communication with Him, as members of His body. And their being so is due to Christ, as well as good for them. His love may well claim this special nearness of them to himself. The fruit of His travail must be very near to His heart and to His hand. He had them in Himself, when they but gave Him all the anguish of His travail; let Him have them in Himself, that His love may be gratified in giving them all the blessings of His purchase.

3. They are "of God" the Father, and they are in Him. They themselves, as elect, were originally of God. The purpose and the scheme of their salvation, and all the provision made for fulfilling that purpose according to that scheme, were of the Father as the representative of Godhead. The Mediator Himself is, as such, of God. His Spirit too cometh from the Father. Thus all they are, and all they receive, as in Christ, must be traced up to God the Father.

And they are in "God the Father" (1 THESS. 1:1). They must be so, because they are in Christ Jesus; for "the Head of Christ is God." He, as the Representative of Godhead, is pledged to secure the effectiveness of Christ's position, as Head by His appointment. "Him hath God the Father sealed." They who are in Christ are thus connected with all the resources of the Godhead. The God of Christ is their God in Christ. Through the relation to the Father of Christ, as the covenant Head, their connection passes in through Christ to God. He who was the Head of Christ for them, according to the promise of the covenant,

IN RELATION TO GOD.

is now their Head through Christ, according to the promise of the Gospel.

The spiritual life of the regenerated is therefore inviolably secure, because of the relation in which, as born again, they stand to the Father, to the Son, and to the Holy Ghost.

II. All who are in Christ are justified; and it is of primary importance to determine in what relation, as justified, they stand to God.

They were guilty sinners under the curse, and ungodly sinners under the yoke, of "the law of works." They were condemned to die, and were excuseless and helpless under the sentence of death; and they were bound to do all that the law required, while lying "without strength" before its broad commandments.

But they are now in Christ, and the righteousness wrought out by Christ, their Surety for them, has been imputed to them by God. Their union to Christ secures this. And it must do so in the first instance; for, as Christ could not procure a right to any blessing of the new covenant for them, except by sealing that covenant with His blood, so, no blessing can be bestowed on them except on the ground of that blood, as placed to their account by God. Christ's fulfilment of the conditions of the covenant must be regarded as theirs in Him, ere the salvation promised to Him for them can actually be theirs. But their union to Christ effectually secures this; for the imputation of the righteousness of Christ, to all who are in Him, is required by the design of God in providing it. "He hath made Him, who knew no sin, to be sin for us, that we might be made the righteousness of God in Him" (2 COR. 5:21). This was God's design; and it must take effect. These are now in Christ, and they must be "made the righteousness of God in Him." And this is due for them to Christ. The Father, as the Divine Sovereign, called Him to the work of righteousness; as Divine Judge, He accepted His work as presented in behalf of those whose substitute He was; and He now owes it to Christ to place it to the account of all who are in Him, and to deal with them according to His merit. Christ, having been "delivered," because their "offences" were laid to His account as their Surety, was raised again because their justification was secured (ROM. 4:25); and the necessary complement of His resurrection is the actual justification of all who are in Him.

Justification, as an act, must be ascribed to God, as Judge; but as a blessing bestowed upon a sinner, it is the gift of God, as Sovereign. As an act, it is a sentence passed in the court of heaven, by God, the Judge of all. True, it is in behalf of a sinner, but that sinner is standing in the right of Christ before the view of God. It respects the righteousness of Christ, as the only ground of it. All it secures is in strict justice due to Christ. He can stand on the merit of His own righteousness, before the throne of God, to claim that this sentence should be passed. But the blessing is intended for the sinner, and he must lie at the footstool of the throne of God the Sovereign, pleading for mercy, while Christ is pleading for the act at the hand of justice before the judgment-seat.

This act of God must be adapted to the state of the sinner in whose behalf, and must accord with the righteousness of Christ on the ground of which, it is done. The sinner is under sentence of death, having been found guilty, and being condemned to die by God as Judge. He is thus liable to the wrath and curse of God; and he is so, as under the administration and according to the terms, of the covenant of works. He can therefore have no right to God's favour, even if he were delivered from God's wrath, unless the law be fulfilled, and, because it has been broken, till it be so fulfilled, as to be "magnified and made honourable." But the righteousness of Christ meets His case; for it includes an atonement by blood for sin, and obedience to the law in fulfilment of the condition of the covenant of works.

The act of God in behalf of such a person, and on the ground of such a righteousness, must therefore secure to him a double benefit, and must have a two-fold effect on that person's relation to God.

1. It must secure a free, full, and final remission of all his guilt—a perfect removal of all that could make him liable to death. This pardon must avail for the removal of all liability to death on account of all the sins which, in relation to the moment in which it is granted, are past, present, and future. It must, (1.) Because it was a loved one who was forgiven, in order to being introduced into a state of grace. I cannot conceive of the love of God being satisfied with less than the gift of such a pardon. (2.) Because all this was due to Christ for him. If Christ procured this for him, the act of justification must have secured this to him; for it was based on His merit. And (3.) Because not otherwise could he be declared entitled to everlasting life. All the sin which exposed him to death, or could do so at any stage of his life, must have been regarded as utterly removed ere a right to eternal life could be given. He could not be accepted unless to this extent forgiven.

Three objections to this doctrine have been advanced.

(1.) That it cannot consist with those scriptures which insist on the necessity of pardon to the justified. (2.) That it tends to antinomianism. And (3.) That the surety righteousness of Christ having been wrought out under the law as a covenant, cannot secure pardon, except of sins committed in breach of the law in its covenant form.

(1.) It is undoubtedly true that the justified do sin, and that because they do, they must ask and receive forgiveness from God; and yet this is quite consistent with the truth that "there is now no condemnation to them who are in Christ Jesus" (ROM. 8:1). Their standing as they are justified, cannot be affected by their sin; for it rests wholly on the righteousness of Christ, and is secured by the irrevocable act of God as Judge declaring them righteous in Christ. They do sin still; and because they are in Christ their sin is all the more aggravated. They do therefore need forgiveness, but not from God as Judge, passing sentence in the court of heaven. They need forgiveness, but it is in the court of conscience, from their Father in heaven (MATT. 6:9,12). His anger has been provoked, and tokens of it are given in the hidings of His face, and in the smitings of His rod. In order to a Fatherly forgiveness, He deals with them by His Word and Spirit, convincing them of sin, and leading them to the blood of Christ, which He applies by faith with the promise of forgiveness anew to their conscience. Their peace with their Father is one thing; their peace with their Judge is another. The former may be often broken, but the latter never can. The former depends on the Spirit's work within them; the latter on Christ's work for them. The one is tasted when God by His Word and Spirit proclaims peace in the court of conscience; the other remains inviolate in the court of heaven. The measure of the one is according to the soul's appreciation and use of the blood of Christ by faith, and flows from the Spirit's work as the Sanctifier; the measure of the other is according to the merit of the blood, as before the mind of God, and results from its imputation to them by the Judge of all.

It is quite true that the pardon of future sins cannot be sealed on the conscience; but may not the believer warrantably expect the remission, by acts of Fatherly forgiveness, of all his future sins? Does not every exercise of the hope of glory imply this? And may he not warrantably conclude, that being already justified, he shall never be again under sentence of death? But that does not prevent his conscience from taking cognisance of his daily sins. While claiming in Christ deliverance from condemnation, he feels that he must ever pray, while he prays at all, "My Father who art in heaven, forgive me my debts, as I forgive my debtors."

(2.) In connection with the "liberty" into which believers "have been called," there is a tendency to "use it for an occasion to the flesh" (GAL. 5:13). This tendency is not in the liberty of their state, nor in the truth of the gospel, but in the old heart. To remove all which it would abuse, would be to take away all privilege and grace. It is a narrow path in which the Christian must walk, between legalism on the one hand, and antinomianism on the other. He should not be enslaved by the fear of condemnation, nor feel and act as if he were not under law to God. His path between these dangers is indeed a narrow one. At neither side may it be broadened. To widen is to destroy it. But God can guide His child therein, and, verily, none other can. It is he who, kept daily sensible of sin, is at the same time standing fast in the liberty wherewith Christ hath made him free, and who, avowing his dependence on the blood, the word, and the Spirit, cries habitually unto his Father for forgiveness, who alone walks freely and warily as becomes a child of God, ready to do his Father's will, and not afraid of lions in the way, having no fear of death, but in constant fear of sinning.

(3.) The question, 'How can the righteousness of Christ meet the guilt of sins committed by the justified?' suggests an objection, not lying against the doctrine of pardon as before stated, so much as against the possibility of these sins being pardoned at all. That righteousness was wrought out under the law, as a covenant, and to meet its claims in that form of its administration. The question then arises, 'How could He, in that position, atone for his people's sins, committed after their deliverance from the covenant of works?' The guilt of these sins must have been atoned for. How otherwise could they be at all forgiven? If atoned for, it must have been by the endurance of the curse of the law as a covenant; and if so, how could such an atonement meet the case of those, who contract guilt after they have ceased to be "under the law?" (ROM. 6:14). The difficulty here is more apparent than real. Christ by His obedience and sufferings met all the claims of the law as a covenant against His people, during all their life on earth. His life-work met all their life-obligations. And they cannot be in Him, without the benefit thus secured to them being acknowledged as theirs by God. They in Him are no longer "under the law," and therefore it can neither condemn them, nor claim from them, as a covenant of works. True, they sin while "under grace"; but in so far as "the law" is concerned, that sin has been already met by the Surety, and disposed of by the Judge.

They are still "under law to God" (1 COR. 9:21). He is their Sovereign and He cannot wink at their sin. He is their Father and He must correct them. Must we desiderate something in the work of Christ, furnishing an immediate and appropriate basis for the dealing of the Sovereign and the Father with the subjects and the children in order to their forgiveness? If so, where shall we find it? Is there aught in the sufferings of Christ that seems specially adapted to meet the sins of the justified? If we could discover in His sufferings, pain that reached Him through another relation than that of Surety, but which affected Him in that position, and therefore formed part of His Surety righteousness, we would seem to have the case fully met. Have we not this in the agony of that hour in which He cried "My God, My God, why hast Thou forsaken me?" It was the Surety of the unjust who uttered this cry, but it was not as Surety He was thus forsaken. It was not *desertion* of which, as Surety, He had painful experience; but of a visit of God in the awfulness of His wrath. It was the presence of God that was terrible to the Surety. Nor was it as Surety He cried "My God, My God." These words expressed His faith as the Father's Servant. They mark His faith's grasp of God in the promise of the covenant. They are His appeal to Him who said, "Behold my servant whom I uphold, mine elect in whom my soul delighteth." As the Father's servant, He was the object of the Father's love. This love was hitherto expressed to Him, as the Servant, in the midst of all His suffering, as the Surety. But the outcome of this love, to the consciousness of Christ, was in this awful hour suspended. He was forsaken. There was a terribly real withdrawal of the light of the Father's face, as the Sovereign whose work Jesus was now bringing to its finish. This came upon Him by His own consent, as well as by the Father's appointment, that in that hour he might specially atone for the sins, by which God's children provoke Him to hide His face from their souls. To His question, "Why hast Thou forsaken me?" no reply was then given. The Spirit of God shall answer it in the hearts and consciences of all the "backsliding children" whom He shall bring back, conscious of sin, and confessing it, to the footstool of their Father's throne. Glorious in His grace and holiness is he, who, on the ground of the agony of Him who was the "Only Begotten," receives that prodigal again, dispels by the light of His countenance the gloom from the face of the guilty, and by His embrace presses out of the wounded spirit the enslaving fear with which felt guilt had filled it.

2. There must be more than pardon in the act of justification—it must declare the person who is justified, entitled to life. This must be involved in it. (1.) Because this is indispensable in order to introduction into a state of grace. There must first be a formal acknowledgement by the Judge, that in reference to this person, the law has been magnified as well as fulfilled; and that thus all has been done in his behalf required to secure, according to the covenant of works, a title to eternal life. Till the law's claims are declared to be met, as well as the demands of avenging justice satisfied, he cannot be placed under the reign of grace, in order to his being preserved unto, and prepared for, the kingdom of heaven. (2.) Because the righteousness of Christ, imputed to him, consists of His obedience to the law, as well as of His atonement by blood for sin to justice. If that righteousness can secure deliverance from death, it must also secure a right to life. An act, expressive of God's estimate of that righteousness, must involve acceptance as well as pardon. This acceptance is an acknowledgement

of the believer's interest in the favour of God—of his right as a subject to the protection of Jehovah, and to the enjoyment of Him as His portion for ever.

The righteousness of Christ secures this on two accounts.(1.) Because it is a fulfilment of the condition of the promise of life, according to the covenant of works. He was "made under the law," in order to atone and to obey, to redeem from death, and to win everlasting life. He has finished His work, and it has been accepted as a fulfilment of the law of works; and, on the ground of it, He can claim life for all who are in Him. (2.) Because of its intrinsic merit. To the merit of Christ's righteousness eternal life is righteously due. His finished work is something altogether unique, as an offering to God. Christ was the only one who could present to God what merits His favour. But He is the Son of God. He is the "fellow" of "the Lord of hosts" (ZECH. 13:7), even while "in the form of a servant." When He lays His work before the throne of God, He can demand an acknowledgement of His claims because of it, from the righteousness of the Judge. He can say "I have glorified thee on the earth," as well as, "I have finished the work which thou gavest me to do." He can demand what He claims as an act of justice, as well as plead for it in fulfilment of promise.

On such ground rests the believer's right to life in Christ. He hath it thus; He hath it at once; His title is already as complete as it shall ever be. The righteousness of Christ merits it; the act of God secures it; the promise of the gospel assures it. "He that believeth, hath everlasting life." He is so related to God, that God is engaged by what He said, by what He did, and by what He is, to protect him by His almighty care, as one entitled to His favour as Lord of all. He is now under divine patronage. God as King, is on His side; and while His reign is effective, the justified can never perish.

As justified, he is for ever free from the yoke of the law as a covenant. All he owed to the law in that form has been paid by his Surety, and has been placed to his account. But he is not, and cannot be "without law to God,"—he is "under law to Christ." As a creature, he must be under the unchanging law of God; and this is the law which is administered by Christ. It has not been modified, as law, to any extent. Its claims have not been abridged. The rule of Christ is the rule of God, and therefore it is righteous and holy. But while the law remains, as such, unchanged, it is administered by Him who is "the Prince of peace," as well as "the mighty God." All God's rights are conserved, and yet the sinful are graciously governed. The name of God is in Him who reigns (EXOD. 23:21); and therefore the will and conscience of the believer must be in subjection to Him; but the King is the High Priest of His people, and pleads His own blood before God in their behalf. And He is their Head. By His Spirit He renews them, and in His grace He gives them strength as they lean on Him by faith. Under such an administration all God's rights are preserved inviolate; and the Divine Ruler, the Mediatorial King, is the Prince of peace to a sinful people.

The result of justification is, not merely the restoration of a man to the relation to God in which Adam originally stood; but his having, on a firmer footing, and with brighter prospects, that position to which Adam would have carried his posterity, if he had fulfilled the condition on which life was promised. And yet the act of adoption is required to constitute the man in Christ a son of God. It is abundantly clear, therefore, that man could not, as created, have been a son of God. Justification does not make him a son, even though he has been regenerated. Adoption still finds a place to complete the status of believers in relation to God; and sanctification, in order to perfect the subjective change, resulting in the child's being, doing and enjoying, all that God, in His love and holiness requires.

III. The act of adoption constitutes a new relation to God. The line of this relation has not hitherto been distinctly traced. This was not done even by such theologians as Calvin, Turretine and Mastricht. The distinction between the result of justification, as affecting the relational status of those who are in Christ, and the peculiar effect of their being adopted as children of God, even those eagles failed to see. Their successors have hitherto added but little to their labours in this department of theology; and notwithstanding a recent discussion, by learned Doctors, of this subject, a clear definition of adoption, and a just description of its effects, on the relation between believers and God, are still awanting.

God is Judge, He is King, He is Father. As Judge, He hath justified the man who is in Christ; and he, having been pardoned and accepted, is passed over under the care of God, as Sovereign, entitled to all the protection He can afford, and having a right to all the enjoyment, which, as a subject, he can have in Jehovah his King. Thus far, and no further, has justification affected his relation to God. But now Jehovah exercises His Sovereignty in a gracious act of adoption, by which He brings the justified one into the relation of a child to Himself. He now becomes his loving Father, as well as his gracious King. He has him now in His house, as well as in His kingdom. He reckons him "among the children" as surely as among the subjects. He hath him, not merely under the protection of His arm, as King, he embraces Him on His bosom as a Father.

We can suppose the case of one under sentence of death, to whom forgiveness has been extended by the king; who, besides, has been declared innocent; and to whom, moreover, a promise has been given, that never again shall he be arrested, tried and condemned. He passes out of prison, to his place as a subject under the protection of the executive government of his country. Special favour is shewn to him even there, and besides all this, by the king. But he is, after all, far from having a child's place in the heart or palace of the sovereign. He is in the house of the king neither as child, nor as courtier, nor as a menial. And although such favour has been shown to him, he is after all, ill-affected towards him to whom he owes so much. His justification did not make him either a child or a loyal loving subject. Ere he could be as near the king as love would crave, and as the king could bring him, he must be adopted; and ere, in the relation of a child or in any other, he could behave becomingly, there must be a change of disposition within him. The points of this analogy indicate the respective places of Justification, Adoption and Sanctification.

Regeneration makes the loved one a living soul; justification removes all that intercepts him from the grace of God; adoption secures to him the place and privileges of a child of God; the Spirit of adoption introduces him in gospel light through Christ to his heavenly Father, and develops in him the disposition of a child; and the Holy Spirit, by His work of sanctification, makes him what his Father would have him to be.

And thus "saith the Scripture"—"God sent forth His Son, made of a woman, made under the law, to redeem them that were under the law, that we might receive the adoption of sons" (GAL. 4:4,5). The first end of Christ's mission is here declared to be, the redemption of His people from the law,—not merely from the curse, but also from the yoke, of the law as a covenant of works. This redemption must have been purchased, ere a right to adoption could have been secured by Christ for His people; and this redemption must have been applied to them, ere they could actually "receive the adoption of sons." They must have been justified on the ground of Christ's imputed righteousness, and thus declared free from the law, ere an act of adoption could introduce them into the place of sons. But they could not be thus justified unless they were in Christ. In Christ they could not be, unless "born, not of blood, nor of the will of the flesh, nor of the will of man, but of God" (JOHN 1:12,13). The act of adoption therefore finds a man already regenerated and justified. These, in the nature of things, must precede, though we cannot antedate them on a line of time.

"Adoption is an act of free grace." It is an expression of the love of God in Christ. This love is a new thing in the manifestation of the divine glory. The display of it is the unique thing in the revelation of

IN RELATION TO GOD.

His name in Christ. His name, as a whole, was glorified as in no other development of His character, but it was in order to the shewing forth of the riches of His grace. It is now that this love can directly touch its object. Till now it was a work of restoration,—a clearing of the ground for a display, in the direct treatment of its object, of this singular love of God. It now finds its object directly before it; and by an act of adoption the loved one becomes a son of God. This is the grand novelty in the adjustment by God according to the covenant of grace, of His people's relational status. "Behold what manner of love the Father hath bestowed on us, that we should be called the sons of God" (1 JOHN 3:1). They are related to Him as His love would have them to be, when they are sons; and no creatures besides are sons as they are.

And Christ has introduced them into their place as sons in the family of God (JOHN 1:12; GAL. 4:4,5). He won it for them; he gives it to them; in Him by faith they find it (GAL. 3:26).

The question, how does Christ give to believers "power to become sons of God" cannot be duly considered in the light of Scripture, without the impression being received, that in some way, and to some extent, the relation of Christ, as Son to God, bears effectively on the relation constituted by adoption. And how does the Sonship of Christ bear upon theirs? Does it only to the extent of securing to Him ability to complete the work of redemption, required in order to their adoption? Farther than this, surely, when we read, "Because ye are sons, God hath sent forth the Spirit of His Son into your hearts." His Sonship tells on them, not merely through their redemption; it bears directly on their standing as adopted. I see it lying back before redemption securing its perfectness, in the light of the words, "God sent forth His Son"; but I see it also directly bearing on them as adopted, when I read, "God hath sent forth the Spirit of His Son into your hearts."

The question to be determined then is, "How does the Sonship of Christ bear on the Sonship of the adopted?" Have they fellowship with Him in that Sonship involved in His relation, as "the only Begotten," to the First Person of the Godhead? This question has recently been discussed by two doctors of divinity. They differed from each other, but they both differed from the truth. They hit different points, but neither hit the mark. The one was right, in so far as he insisted that the Sonship of Christ affects the relation which adoption constitutes. The other was right, in so far as he denied the identity of the Sonship, constituted by the eternal generation of the Second Person of the Godhead, with that which results from adoption. Beyond this they have contributed nothing to the settlement of this question. Principal Candlish ignores Christ's federal relation to His Father and to His people; and applies to Him, as the Second Person of the Godhead, passages which refer to Him only as the federal head of the redeemed; the truth being, that *the Sonship of Christ cannot affect the sonship of the adopted, except so far as it affects His own relations and power as the Christ of God.* Dr. Crawford fails to perceive any bearing of Christ's Sonship on the relation formed by adoption; and commits the flagrant blunder of ascribing a sonship to Christ's human nature, distinct from that which pertains to Him because of His eternal generation.

The key for opening this question is given in GAL. 4:6. The Son is sent to secure "the adoption of sons" to His people. This He does by redeeming them. Redemption having been applied to them, so that they are justified, they "receive the adoption of sons." And because they are—not that they might be—sons, they receive "the Spirit of the Son." Now, in order to apprehend how Christ's relation to God affects that of the adopted, we must determine what that relation had been before His mission, what it was while He was engaged in His work, and what it became when His work was finished. It is only this last that can tell directly and effectively on the status of His people.

Viewed as coming, He is recognised as the Son of God. Eternally Begotten of the Father, He is therefore His Son. He is eternal and yet Begotten; and as Begotten He is the well beloved Son. He who came was the Covenant Head. He "was set up" as such "from everlasting." He engaged by promise to the Father, as the representative of Godhead, to implement the conditions of the covenant of grace; and He is come to fulfil His promise. He came, and yet He is where He was. He who is the Son of man on the earth is still "in heaven" (JOHN 3:13). He vacates not His place, as a divine person, on the throne of God, nor His place, as Son, in the bosom of the Father.

The sent Son is "made of a woman." The *person* "made of a woman" is "the Son." His human nature born of a woman, can have no distinct Sonship, for it subsists in the Person of the Son of God, and must participate in the Sonship of that Person. His flesh was not first formed and then united to the Godhead. It never had existed apart from the Person of the Son. *"The Son"* was "made of a woman,"—not His human nature apart from Him—and now "in the flesh," He who is the Son and the Christ of God is before us.

But Messiah in the flesh on earth is the Father's *Servant.* He is engaged in a work which the Father gave Him to do. His relation as Servant, is to the Father as representing the sovereignty of the Godhead, and having to provide for the fulfilment of the divine purpose of salvation. The Servant must be subject to Him who sent Him. He has received commandment from the Father, and He is obedient. And He must be upheld by Him who sent Him. He is the Son, and

IN RELATION TO GOD.

hath as His own, all the resources of the Godhead; but He, in "the form of a servant," denies Himself to the independent use of these. He is willing to depend on Him who sent Him. His Godhead secures that He shall willingly occupy such a position. To do so is a fitting expression of divine zeal, instead of being inconsistent with divine power. A scheme that is divine must be avowedly executed at the expense of Him who represents the Godhead. The Father is God representatively; and the Son, as His Servant, lives by Him who sent Him, in the faith of the promise given to Him in the covenant.

The promised service was to act the part of a *Surety* for His people. He was accordingly "made under the law,"—His being made of a woman did not imply this. His human nature was not necessarily under law, for it had no personal subsistence apart from the Godhead; and it is with a person, and not with a nature the law has to do. But this Person, who was "made of a woman," was the Son of God. Ere He could be under the law, He must have, by a Sovereign exercise of His own will, subjected Himself to it, according to the appointment of the Father. As Surety He is related to God as Judge. From Him now "under the law," as His people's Surety, God as Judge demands all that is required, of obedience in order to the law being magnified, and of suffering in order to justice being satisfied.

In the form of a Servant, and in the position of a Surety, the Son could not display the dignity, and enjoy the blessedness, proper to Him, as the only Begotten of the Father. He was "a man of sorrows" then. But He was the Son, even when "learning obedience," as Servant, "by the things which He suffered," as Surety.

The result of His work, as Servant, being finished is, that His obligations, as Surety, are discharged. He must be no longer "in the form of a servant"; He must be no longer "under the law." The Judge sets the Surety free; the King comes in His glory to honour His Servant; and the Father receives into His bosom His Son in the flesh. He emerges now out of servitude and sorrow, into His glory and blessedness, as the Son of God. But he rises as His people's Head. As such He passes into His place as Son, in order that the power of His position as "Son over His own house" may be exercised in their behalf; and that His relation, as the Son to the Father, may affect their relation through Him, as their Head, to God.

The Sonship of the risen Head, *as representing power and intimacy with God,* must affect the relation to God of the members of His body. It may not be right to say that He has a mediatorial Sonship distinct from the divine; it may be better to conceive of Him as entering as His people's Head, in their nature, into His place as the Eternal Son of God (JOHN 17:5), in order that He may wield all the power of that position as the "Prince and Saviour" of His people. He in the flesh is reigning in His place as Son; and He reigns there as His people's Head. He is "a Son over His own house." This Sonship represents His mediatorial sovereignty. "Kiss ye the Son," is Jehovah's claim in behalf of Zion's King. To declare Him Son, by His resurrection from the dead, was to crown Him King. Christ exalted in human nature to the place of the Son, must be a King. A careful study of the second psalm should suffice to convince any unprejudiced mind, that the Sonship of Christ, as exalted in human nature, represents His Kingly power, as His people's Head. It is only in this light we can understand the words, referring to the end of all things, "When He shall have delivered up the kingdom to God," "then shall the Son also Himself be subject unto Him that put all things under Him, that God may be all in all." This cannot apply to Him as the eternal Son of God, for as such He and the Father are one; it can only mean that, at the end of all things, the mediatorial government shall be merged in the divine.

Now I cannot trace the course of Christ from His place as servant and surety in the flesh on earth, up to His position of power and glory as the Son on high, and keep in view throughout His relation to His people, without expecting as the result, an analogous transition of all His members, from bondage and insecurity, as the servants of sin, into the liberty and steadfastness of the position of sons in the Father's house. He was for them, in the position of a servant. He was made under the law, and He was "made sin," and He was "made a curse," and He died. He was thus associated with them in servitude. But not as they were there, was He. He was much that they could not be; even though under their very yoke, and bearing their very sins. He partook of "flesh and blood," and thus He and they "were all of one." He in His person as Emmanuel, bridged the great chasm, between them in their meanness and Jehovah in His majesty, becoming their Brother, while remaining the "fellow" of "the Lord of hosts." But what a difference there was in the mode of His servitude as compared with theirs! And if they now associate with Him in the Sonship to which He is exalted, as their risen Head, the difference between Him and them, must mark a corresponding difference in the mode of His Sonship, as compared with theirs. Sons they shall be, because He, as their Head, is Son; but not as He is, can they be sons.

The Head is now in the Son's place, and His people are one with Him. Are they not, therefore, it may be asked, introduced into the self-same relation to God which His Sonship indicates? No; and just because it is as their Head He is there, they cannot be sons as He is Son. They are in Him; but only as His members. He is the only Head. Their position in the Father's house as sons must therefore be subordinate. He, being the Head, is alone where He is; but He gives to them all which, in that relation, He hath to bestow, and which they can receive. I must not aspire to be a son as He is, nor must I aspire to His position as the exalted Head. But I cannot be one with Him who is the Head, and who as the Head is Son, without being a son myself. But I must owe this to redeeming grace; and I can receive it only by an act of adoption. His relation to God, as my Head, secured my sonship, but, being a member, I cannot share His with Him who alone is Head. To exercise His power as Son, in giving me fellowship in His own Sonship, would be as inconsistent with the scheme of redemption, as with the utter incommunicableness of a Sonship constituted by eternal generation. This is forbidden by what God has arranged in the everlasting covenant, as well as by what God is in the Trinity of persons. He has reserved the place of Head for His Son; and although Christ and His people are brethren, He shall for ever be "the only Begotten Son of God."

How then does the Son make believers free? How does He give "to as many as receive Him power to become the sons of God"? It cannot be by His sharing His own Sonship with them. If He had not higher Sonship than any He could share with them, never could He have made them sons at all. Though Son, as none but He can ever be, He became for them a servant. But in their nature, in which He served, and by serving and suffering redeemed them, He rose again to the place of power and glory which is His as Son. He went down for them and He rose for them. He raised up His redeemed, to His place on high, in Himself their risen Head. On the footing, on which His position rests, as their Head in the Father's house, is theirs as His members. They are free and they are sons in Him. Eternal as His life on high is theirs. He has introduced them as His members, in His own right, as raised to the place of Son, to His God and Father. He claims for them all His God's provision, He claims for them all His Father's love; but He claims this for them as redeemed creatures. As God, eternally begotten, He is Son; as creatures, redeemed and adopted, they are sons. But all He is, as Son, gives strength to the basis of their position, and His intimacy as the Son with His Father, is the medium of their communion with God for ever. And He gives to them the Spirit as well as the privilege of adoption. The Spirit of adoption is the Spirit of the Son. He hath power to send Him, now that He is in the Son's place on high, and the Spirit comes to give to them the enjoyment of what is theirs in union with the Son.

"I ascend unto my Father and your Father, and to my God and your God" (JOHN 20:17), was Christ's way of announcing His ascension to His disciples. Thus He would teach them, that His relation to the

Father secured a corresponding relation for them. But He does not say that it is His own Sonship which is shared by them. He does assure them that His God would be theirs, because all He hath from the Father, as their Head, would be theirs in Him. He tells them, too, that His Father would be their Father, because He their Head would receive, in the acknowledgement of His Sonship in the flesh, a pledge of theirs by adoption, and they in Him would "be called the sons of God." But He does not say "Our Father" as if He and they stood on the same level in relation to God as sons. "My Father" is "your Father," but not as He is mine is He yours. Being mine He is yours; for having received me, your Head, into the glory of the Son, He must adopt all who are in me, and acknowledge them as sons.

And He promises a place on His throne, at last, to all who are the sons of God (REV. 3:21). This may seem, at first sight, as if it implied the identity of their ultimate standing in the Father's house, with that of Christ Himself. But, examined more closely, the terms of His promise are seen to teach the very opposite. He speaks of His own seat on the Father's throne. This is a pledge of their victory and enthronement. But He does not promise them a place on the Father's throne. He alone is there as "the Only Begotten Son." It is in His own throne they shall find their place. True, His is the Father's throne; but it is His alone. They are not to share it with Him, as the Eternal Son. It is on the throne which is His own, as their Head, He shall give them a place.

In those passages in which Christ speaks of the Father's loving His people as He loved Himself, He can only refer to the Father's love to Himself as Mediator. It is undoubtedly to that love He refers, when He saith, "Therefore doth my Father love me, because I lay down my life that I might take it again" (JOHN 10:17). He, as the Mediator who engaged to glorify the name, and to fulfil the purpose of the Father, and who presented in His person all that was required for the success of His undertaking, was the object of the Father's love. This love found expression in His own exaltation in human nature, to "the glory" which He had, as Son, with the Father "before the foundation of the world" (JOHN 17:5,24). And this love shall, through him, be expressed in all that shall be given, for His sake, and out of His fulness, to all the members of His body.

It is not necessary to intrude our conceptions within the precincts of deity, in order to apprehend, as a position of dignity and grace ineffable, that of those who are sons by adoption. They shall rank as creatures for ever; and their consciousness of being so shall only enhance their blessedness, as they commune as sons with Jehovah, and serve Him for ever.

IN RELATION TO GOD.

They are sons indeed, though not sons as is the Second Person of the Godhead. All that is desirable they enjoy, while having only what is legitimate. Infinitely beneath Jehovah's "Only Begotten" in rank, and having fellowship with Him only in what is His as Mediator, how inestimable is their privilege, and how high their rank, in their relation, as adopted, to the Father, to the Son, and to the Holy Ghost.

1. To the Father, to whom they ultimately owe all they are and have as sons, and to whom the line of their relation, as sons, must be ultimately traced. He "predestinated" them "unto the adoption of children by Jesus Christ to Himself" (EPH. 1:5). But the love which moved Him so to purpose was peculiar love to "a peculiar people." The results of that love must present a novelty amidst all the arrangements and works of God. The Sonship flowing from it must be a new thing. It cannot be such as that of the Only Begotten; and it cannot be such as that of the angels who "kept their first estate." It is the fruit of God's love to sinners through a Mediator. Those who are saved by grace must hold a unique position. The line of their relation must start from the level of a creature's rank, and from within the mediatorial sphere. The line of the Eternal Son's relation to the Father is throughout within the divine circle; but that of the adopted must be traced from creature status, through the Mediator, up to God. They shall never be deified; therefore they never can be sons, as is the Second Person of the Godhead.

But they are sons indeed. Jehovah hath arranged for their being so—mean, loathsome, hostile, guilty though they were,—so that He may be glorified in being their Father, and that they, not only can endure, but find perfect blessedness in, being sons of God. He meets them in the Mediator, and while appearing in the manifested glory of all His name, He, by an act of Adoption, takes them into His family. He becomes their Father. He pledges Himself to a fatherly loving treatment of them. And all He is as God gives security for the perfect fatherliness of His love and dealing.

How strange it is that the High and Lofty One who inhabiteth Eternity, and whose name is Holy, should have such sons as these! How wonderful it is that they, who, while on earth, have all sin within them, could taste the fatherly love of Him who "is a consuming fire"! But He is their Father, and He loves them; and they are His children, and they cry, 'Abba, Father.' And all the more ravishing is their enjoyment of His love, when they recognise their Father as the High, the Eternal, and the Holy One. But how distant must their communion with Him be while they are on earth—while that "body of death" is in them! Dark hours of felt desertion, and dead hours of silence, they shall often have while here. Often shall they be smitten; for chastisement must be the expression of a Father's love to backsliding children (HEB. 12:6). Stern love it seems, if love at all, which the strokes of the rod express; and hard thoughts do start up in the heart, as stripe after stripe is felt. But He is a Father then, though the afflicted child suspects Him—a divine Father, infinite in love and faithfulness. Just because He is "God and Father," He must meantime keep His adopted children at a distance. They are sinners; and they are of a race that must be propagated through successive generations on the earth. They may thus have forty years of a wilderness life, during which evil still remains within them, and throughout which distant, dim, and broken shall be their glimpses of their Father's glory, and brief their tastings of their Father's grace. Till they cease to be sinful, they cannot cease to be afflicted; and till they be perfectly holy, they cannot be "with the Lord" (1 PET. 1:15,16). But He will have them to be holy, and His Fatherly love shall be gratified. The Almighty cannot be disappointed in His sons. There is a guarantee divinely strong for their perfect holiness, and therefore for their perfect bliss.

How safe in the house of God are these adopted ones! He took them in when they were at their worst. He proclaimed Himself their Father then. His zeal for His own glory, as well as His love to them, requires that not one of them should perish; and makes it certain that all of them shall yet be all that the sons of God should be, that their Father's love may be gratified, and His name glorious for ever.

2. To the Son. It was the Father's purpose to bring all His elect as sons to glory (HEB. 2:10). They were partakers of flesh and blood; and the Son, who undertook the fulfilment of the Father's purpose, became incarnate that He might thus become their Brother. "The children" are thus the brethren of the man who is the "Fellow" of "the Lord of hosts." His Son, remaining all He was, is now a brother to the objects of His love; and if God may condescend to adopt the brethren of His Only Begotten, they may approach through Him to God. The Only Begotten as their Brother, can act the part of a Redeemer for them, that it may become the character, as well as consist with the rank, of Jehovah, to make them sons by adoption. He, passing to the Father's house, after His life and death as a man of sorrows on the earth, can have a brother's sympathy with them during all their life of trial. And in the Father's house at last, He shall act the elder brother's part, in leading them "to the living fountains of water."

And He is their living Head. In Him they have redemption; in Him they are sons. They are legally one with Him as their Surety, who hath sealed the covenant with His blood; and they are vitally connected with Him as the Head in whom all fullness dwelleth. He as their Surety took a position once, between which and the Son's place on high, lay the wrath and curse of God, and the broad commandments of the law; He served and suffered His way on through all, till, death and resurrection past, He at last entered on His glory. He bore them in Himself through all, and hath them now as a redeemed inheritance in "the heavenly places." One after another has been actually "quickened together with Christ," and has actually in person entered into His rights as the Covenant Head. Their footing now is His for them. He passed, into His place as Son, in the flesh and for them—as their Kinsman and their Head. He hath thus secured their sonship; and while He is where He now is, their position as sons is secure. The Son has made them free, and they are "free indeed" (JOHN 8:35,36).

And He is the First-born above them all. He is the only Son who is "over the house of God." He holds a Prince's place over all besides. Near indeed to Jehovah is He—He is Himself Jehovah—and sweet to them it is to come through Him nigh to God. But they are subject to Him while they are one spirit with Him. To the divine in Him they must render homage, even while leaning on His kinship. A brother's intimacy they may enjoy, but divine majesty they must adore. They may come near to Him, but they must worship as they approach Him.

And they shall all be like Him. The Elder Brother, "the man Christ Jesus," is the model before the eye of all the sons. Like Him they all desire to be; and perfectly like Him shall they all become. They were "predestinated to be conformed to the image of the Son" (ROM. 8:29); and they "beholding as in a glass the glory of the Lord, are changed into the same image" (2 COR. 3:18); and "when He shall appear they shall be like Him," for they "shall see Him as He is" (1 JOHN 3:2). Their soul shall be perfectly conformed to His; and their risen body shall be "fashioned like to His glorious body." Oh, what a consummation! How delightful to the Father! how satisfying to the sons! Before the Father shall the Elder Brother present the children all, in the beauty of His likeness. How certain and how fervent shall their welcome be from God! How sure is a mansion for each of them in the Father's house! How ravishing their bliss as they shall dwell there for ever! But verily, "it doth not yet appear what" they "shall be."

3. To the Holy Ghost; who as "the Spirit of the Son" is in their very hearts. By Him they receive all they get from their Father, through the Elder Brother. He is with them to conduct a meet and effective patronage of them, with all their failings, amid all their trials, and during all their life on earth. Hidden, indeed, is His presence "in the inner man." Often must He touch and teach them, to make them aware of the divine displeasure, because of their many sins. Seldom does He impress a sense of His presence, in felt and fervent love, on their consciousness. He acts as becomes the Holy One in carrying on His work

of grace. He must be "a consuming fire" to the sin which pollutes them, as well as a Comforter to themselves. But how fatherly, notwithstanding, is God's way of dealing with them by His Spirit! Because they are sons, they are kept from the utter torpor of feeling, under which others lie insensate. Their very groanings, under the burden of corruption, tell that they are sons, and that a Father's hand is on them. It is the support of a Father's arm that has kept them from sinking in the deeps through which they passed. How often would they utterly faint, unless He graciously revived them! These calm moments of renewed peace, these glimpses of the King in His beauty, and of the land that is far off, these free movements in the ways of God, these triumphs over sin in its mighty lustings, and over Satan with his mighty hosts, are surely tokens of a Father's love—the foretastes of such rest and happiness at last, as shall leave to the child no more to desire, and to the Father no more to bestow.

Index To Subjects

ABOUNDING SIN, 63.
Act Of Creation, 12.
Act Of Grace, 22.
Adam, 13, 18, 19, 22, 23, 24, 29, 30, 31, 33, 34, 37, 42, 62, 71.
Adamic Covenant, 18, 29, 30, 31.
Adam, "The Son Of God," 13, 19.
Adoption, 22, 23, 38, 60, 70, 72, 73, 74, 76, 77, 78, 79, 80.
Adopting Grace, 19.
Alliance To God, 12.
Antinomianism, 66, 67.
Apostles, 36.
Arminian, 51, 52, 53, 55, 56, 57.
Atonement For Sin, 41, 56.

BACKSLIDING CHILDREN, 69, 80.
Believers, 37, 38, 56, 58, 59, 67, 71, 73, 75.
Blood For Sin, 66, 69.

CALL OF THE GOSPEL, 47, 51, 57.
Calvin, 71.
Calvinist, 45, 50, 51, 53, 55, 56.
Calvinistic Formula, 25.
Candlish, 19, 73.
Catholic, 37, 38.
Child Of Adam, 19, 30, 37.
Child Of God, 21, 24, 68, 69, 71, 72.
Child Of Wrath, 28, 29, 33.
Children, 21, 23, 25, 32, 68, 79, 80, 81.
Christ The Son Of God, 32.
Communion With God, 22, 77.
Condemnation, 67.
Condemned, 30, 33, 65, 66, 72.
Condescension Of God, 12, 63.
Confession of Faith, 51, 53, 54, 55, 57.
Conscience, 15, 28, 49, 51, 55, 67, 69, 70.
Conscious of Sin, 69.
Covenant Love Of God, 53.
Covenant Of Grace, 32, 33, 34, 35, 41, 42, 49, 58, 61, 62, 73, 74.

Covenant Of Works, 18, 22, 29, 30, 31, 32, 35, 37, 62, 66, 68, 69, 70, 72.
Creation, 12, 14, 15, 19, 21, 22, 24, 25.
Creator, 11, 12, 13, 14, 18, 19, 21, 29.

DEED OF GIFT AND GRANT, 57, 58.
Definition Of Adoption, 71.
Dependence Upon God, 14.
Dispensation Of Providence, 18.
Divine Glory, 28, 38, 42, 57, 72.
Divine Holiness, 22, 28.
Divine Love, 43, 45, 46, 58, 61.
Divine Power, 16, 63, 75.
Divine Ruler, 71.
Divinely Arranged Ritual, 39.
Double Reference Of The Atonement, 51, 53, 54, 55, 56.
Dr. Crawford, 24, 74.
Duty, 37, 57.

ELECTING LOVE OF GOD, 34, 43.
Eternal Son Of God, 75, 76.
Evil, 13, 15, 17, 27, 28, 80.
Evil and Unthankful, 21.
Evil As An Abstraction, 17.

FATHER'S HOUSE, 76, 77, 78, 80, 81.
Fatherhood Of God, 19, 24, 25, 31.
Fatherly Love Of God, 25, 31.
Favour Of God, 22, 70.
Federal Head, 18, 33, 61, 64, 74.
Federal Relation, 73.
Federal Union, 33.
First Sin, 30.
Forsaking God, 14.

GERM OF ALL HOLINESS, 61.
Gift of His Son, 23.
Glorious Grace, 34.
God And Adam, 18.
God And Man, 18, 19.
God As Judge, 16, 66, 67, 75.
God Is Holy, 22.
God May Justify The Ungodly, 16.
God The Father, 22, 52, 62, 64.

Index To Subjects

God The Holy Ghost, 22.
God's Authority As Judge, 17.
God's Children, 69.
God's Grace, 35.
God's Right To Reign, 17.
God's Sovereignty, 18, 20, 34, 41, 42, 71, 74.
God's Spiritual Being, 14.
God's Will, 17, 18.
God's Work, 11, 14, 48, 79.
God's Worthiness, 16.
Good For All, 52.
Good For Some, 52.
Goodness Of God, 21, 44.
Guilt, 66, 68, 69.
Guilty, 17, 27, 28, 34, 36, 43, 51, 56, 65, 66, 69, 79.

HEAVEN, 11, 16, 36, 38, 50, 65, 67.
Hell, 16, 38, 45, 62.
Holiness, 38, 80.
Honour Of His Law, 37.

IMAGE OF GOD, 11, 12, 22, 27, 28, 37.
Image Of The Son, 81.
Imputed Sin, 32, 53, 56.
In Adam, 23, 33.
In Christ, 22, 33, 35, 42, 44, 45, 46, 48, 49, 58, 61, 62, 64, 65, 67, 70, 71, 72.
Insensate Hearts, 31.
Irrevocable Act Of God, 67.

JESUS CHRIST, 22, 23, 25, 32, 41, 44, 46, 48.

KINGDOM, 76.
Kingdom Of God, 62, 71.
Kingdom Of Heaven, 54, 69.

LAW OF CHRIST, 59.
Likeness Unto God, 22.
Love Of God, 22, 23, 25, 43, 44, 45, 46, 47, 48, 66, 72, 73.

MAN A SON OF GOD, 22.
Man And God Before The Fall, 19.

Man In Eden, 12, 21, 36.
Man In Heaven, 16.
Man's Promise To God, 18.
Mastricht, 71.
Mediator, 16, 23, 36, 54, 61, 63, 64, 78, 79.
Mediatorial, 25, 36, 64, 71, 75, 76, 78, 79.
Mind Of God, 18, 33, 34, 47, 52, 67.
Moral Law, 15, 16, 20, 30, 37.

NAME OF GOD, 38, 47, 58, 70.
Nature Of God, 25.
Non-Elect, 46.

OFFER, 56, 57.
Offspring Of God The Creator, 19.
Old Testament God, 42.
Omnipresence Of God, 12.
Only Begotten Son Of God, 77.

PERFECT OBEDIENCE TO GOD, 18.
Power Of God, 12, 13, 62, 63.
Power Of Satan, 28, 62.
Power Of Sin, 30.
Presence Of God, 17, 62, 69.
Promises Of Grace, 39.

RESPONSIBILITY, 15, 18, 30.
Restoration of Man, 22.
Revealed Will Of God, 37, 50.

SACRIFICE FOR SIN, 50.
Satan, 27, 28, 62, 63, 82.
Saving Grace, 44, 50.
Saviour, 24, 39, 40, 41, 46, 47, 48, 49, 51, 57.
Scheme Of Grace, 31, 35, 39, 42.
Sense Of Sin, 41.
Sensible Of Sin, 68.
Sermon On The Mount, 24, 59.
Sermons, 36, 58, 59.
Servants Of Sin, 76.
Sin And Misery, 32.
Sin Before The Mind Of God, 34.
Sin Is Enmity To God, 28.
Sin Takes Possession, 28.

Index To Subjects

Sin Was Charged, 54.
Sin Which Pollutes, 82.
Slave Of Sin, 28.
Sons By Adoption, 78, 80.
Sons Of God, 78, 79, 80.
Sovereign Grace, 19, 23.
Spirit Of Adoption, 38, 72, 77.
Spirit Of Christ, 36.
Spirit Of God, 28, 34, 57, 62, 69.
Spirit Of Grace, 34.
Spirit Of Life, 64.
Spirit Of The Son, 38, 74, 77, 81.
Spirit Proclaims Peace, 67.
State Of Grace, 34, 64, 66, 69.
Subject Of God, 16.
Subjection To God, 13, 18.
Sufferings Of Jesus Christ, 25.
Sway Of Sin, 28.

THE FALL, 19, 25, 27, 28, 36.
The Quickener, 62.
The Sanctifier, 62, 67.
Turretine, 71.

UNBELIEVERS, 37, 58.
Universal Fatherhood, 23, 24, 25, 31.
Universal Grace, 55, 56.
Universal Reference Of The Atonement, 52, 53, 56, 57.

WAGES OF SIN, 30.
Wisdom Of God, 18.
Word Of God, 23, 25, 45, 53.
Work Of God, 11, 48.
Work Of Grace, 22, 35, 46, 51, 63, 81.
Wrath, 13, 17, 18, 27, 29, 31, 32, 33, 42, 43, 47, 55, 66, 69.
Wrath And Curse Of God, 66, 81.

Index To Scripture References

OLD TESTAMENT

Gen. 1:11 11
Gen. 2:7 12
Gen. 12:3 38

Exod. 23:20,21 36
Exod. 23:21 70
Exod. 34:6,7 42

Num. 16:22 13

Psa. 50:6 16
Psa. 115:16 11
Psa. 148:14 23

Isa. 9:6 64
Isa. 43:21 11
Isa. 45:9 13
Isa. 45:17 39

Jer. 23:6 39

Ezek. 36:26,27 61

Zech. 13:7 70

Mal. 2:10 24

NEW TESTAMENT

Matt. 5:11,12 24
Matt. 5:13,14 24
Matt. 5:45 21
Matt. 6:9,12 67
Matt. 11:25 25
Matt. 11:25,26 33
Matt. 28:19 39

Luke 3:38 . . . . 19, 23
Luke 15 23
Luke 24:16 36
Luke 24:27 36
Luke 24:31 36

John 1:4 14
John 1:12 . . . . 22, 73
John 1:12,13 . . . . 62, 72
John 1:14 37
John 3:3 62
John 3:13 74
John 3:16 . . . . 22, 53
John 3:36 62
John 6 58
John 6:27 58
John 6:29 58
John 6:32 58
John 6:35 58
John 6:37 49
John 6:39 . . . . 34, 58
John 6:40 49
John 6:44 59
John 6:51 58
John 6:69 48
John 8:35,36 81
John 8:36 38
John 10:10 23
John 10:17 78
John 15:26 61
John 16:7 61
John 17:5 75
John 17:5,24 78
John 20:17 77

Acts 2:16 36
Acts 2:22-36 47
Acts 17:28 . . . . 11, 19
Acts 17:28,29 23

Rom. 1:3 40
Rom. 2:3 30
Rom. 2:5 29
Rom. 2:15 28
Rom. 3:20 30
Rom. 4:25 65
Rom. 5:8 53
Rom. 5:20 23
Rom. 6:14 68
Rom. 7:8 30
Rom. 7:10 18
Rom. 8:1 67
Rom. 8:15 38
Rom. 8:29 81
Rom. 8:32 53
Rom. 9 33
Rom. 9:4 23

Index To Scripture References

Rom. 9:11 33
Rom. 11:7-10 46
Rom. 16:26 37

1 Cor. 1:23 40
1 Cor. 6:19 62
1 Cor. 9:21 . . . . 37, 68
1 Cor. 11:3 64

2 Cor. 3:18 81
2 Cor. 5:14 50
2 Cor. 5:18 64
2 Cor. 5:21 . . . . 53, 65
2 Cor. 6:16 62
2 Cor. 6:18 21

Gal. 3:8 35
Gal. 3:10 30
Gal. 3:24 37
Gal. 3:26 73
Gal. 4:6 . . . . 38, 74
Gal. 4:4,5 . . . . 72, 73
Gal. 5:13 67
Gal. 5:17 62
Gal. 5:25 62

Eph. 1:5 79
Eph. 1:6 23
Eph. 1:7 51
Eph. 2:1-3 28
Eph. 2:4,5 61
Eph. 2:14 38

Col. 1:21 28

1 Thess. 1:1 64

Heb. 2:10 80
Heb. 2:11 33
Heb. 2:16 34
Heb. 8:8-13 37
Heb. 9:14 50
Heb. 10:19,20 38
Heb. 12:6 80
Heb. 12:9 23

1 Pet. 1:11 36
1 Pet. 1:15,16 80

1 Pet. 1:25 36

1 John 2:2 53
1 John 3:1 72
1 John 3:2 81

Rev. 3:21 78